The Academic
Chair's Handbook

Daniel W. Wheeler
Alan T. Seagren
Linda Wysong Becker
Edward R. Kinley
Dara D. Mlinek
Kenneth J. Robson

The Academic Chair's Handbook

Second Edition

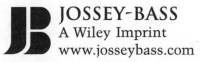

JOSSEY-BASS
A Wiley Imprint
www.josseybass.com

Published by Jossey-Bass
A Wiley Imprint
989 Market Street, San Francisco, CA 94103–1741   www.josseybass.com

Jossey-Bass books and products are available through most bookstores. To contact Jossey-Bass directly call our Customer Care Department within the U.S. at 800-956-7739, outside the U.S. at 317-572-3986, or fax 317-572-4002.

Jossey-Bass also publishes its books in a variety of electronic formats. Some content that appears in print may not be available in electronic books.

Library of Congress Cataloging-in-Publication Data

The academic chair's handbook / Daniel W. Wheeler . . . [et al.]. — 2nd ed.
        p. cm.
    Rev. ed. of: The academic chairperson's handbook. c1990.
    Includes bibliographical references and indexes.
    ISBN 978-0-470-19765-3 (cloth)
        1. College department heads—United States—Handbooks, manuals, etc.
    2. Universities and colleges—United States—Departments—Handbooks, manuals, etc. 3. College teachers—United States. I. Wheeler, Daniel W., 1939-

    LB2341.A217 2008
    378.1'11—dc22   2007049751

Printed in the United States of America
SECOND EDITION
HB Printing 10 9 8 7 6 5 4 3 2 1

Contents

About the Authors

Daniel W. Wheeler is professor and head of the Department of Agricultural Leadership, Education, and Communication at the University of Nebraska–Lincoln. He has conducted research on chairs and departments and has provided workshops for chairs and other administrators for more than 20 years.

Alan T. Seagren is professor emeritus and director of the Center for the Study of Higher and Postsecondary Education at the University of Nebraska–Lincoln. He has been a faculty member, chair and dean, and senior administrator in both academic and business affairs. His research has focused on chairs and departments, and he has provided seminars and workshops to chairs and other administrators.

Linda Wysong Becker is the vice president for student services at Union College and former director of human resources at Andrews University. She completed her doctorate at the University of Nebraska–Lincoln in higher education administration with an emphasis in leadership. Her areas of special interest are leadership and continuous improvement, and she has been a Baldrige examiner.

Edward R. Kinley is associate vice president for academic affairs and chief information officer at Indiana State University. He has extensive experience as an administrator, teacher, and information technology specialist and has worked in both the public and private sectors.

Dara D. Mlinek received her doctorate and master's degrees from the University of Nebraska–Lincoln. She was a research assistant and instructor in the Center for the Study of Higher and Postsecondary Education and participated in the center's research efforts focused on chairs.

Kenneth J. Robson began his career as a faculty member and has served as a department chair, dean, and vice president. He also provides leadership training for academic administrators both nationally and internationally. He is currently engaged in a higher education consulting practice with his partner, J. Judith Eifert, who also served as a faculty member and administrator in several senior capacities.

Foreword

It has long been the custom in colleges and universities to prevail upon faculty who have been trained to teach and conduct research in their areas of specialization to assume administrative roles for which they have neither the training nor the experience. Those who accept frequently view themselves as scholars who, out of a sense of duty, temporarily take on responsibility for administrative tasks in order to reduce the burden on colleagues who are intent on pursuing their teaching and research interests.

However, it has become increasingly evident that the current environment of higher education is far too complex and demanding for such an approach to remain effective. Clearly, with nearly 50,000 scholars in the United States alone presently serving as department chairs, and almost one-quarter having to be replaced each year, much more needs to be done to provide adequate preparation and support to these key academic leaders.

Although there is no shortage of business literature exhorting managers to become more effective leaders or extolling the virtues of legendary leaders whose practices should be emulated, there have been relatively few works to guide academic leaders, and especially department chairs. As recently as two decades ago the only book available to guide chairs was Allan Tucker's classic work funded by the Kellogg Foundation, *Chairing the Academic Department* (1981). However, it was not until the first edition of *The Academic Chair-*

person's Handbook (1990), researched and written by some of the current edition's authors, that the field of academic leadership finally received a data-based study that translated research into practice. Rather than merely speculate on the challenges confronting department chairs and prescribe the preferred ways of dealing with them, the authors chose to conduct in-depth interviews with 200 chairs on 70 college and university campuses across the United States. What emerged from their research was a distillation of 15 key leadership strategies augmented by excerpts from the interviews, which provided both a context for and a rich texture to the strategies themselves. Remarkably, the *Handbook* provided for the first time an opportunity to view the lived experience of these front-line academic leaders.

The welcome appearance of this extensively revised edition of the *Handbook* confirms both the perennial challenges associated with academic leadership and the emergence of new issues in recent years. What the current generation of chairs, to whom this latest edition of the *Handbook* is addressed, require, in my view, is assistance in developing competence in three major areas: 1) a conceptual understanding of the unique roles and responsibilities encompassed by academic leadership; 2) the skills necessary to achieve results through working with faculty, staff, students, and other administrators; and 3) the practice of reflection that enables one to learn from past experiences in order to perfect the art of leadership.

What I mean by a *conceptual understanding* of academic leadership is the ability to understand the role within its unique context. This is essentially a cognitive exercise that entails an understanding of mental models, frameworks, and role theory. Two issues are important in this regard: 1) as faculty move into leadership positions, the concept of what it means to be an academic shifts; and 2) institutions of higher education face unique challenges that are not typical of those faced by their counterparts in other types of organizations. Colleges and universities most often operate through influence and indirection rather than through any kind of command

and control structure. Their products, processes, and customers are often ill-defined and subject to quite different interpretations. The *Handbook* not only addresses the critical question of how to understand and respond to traditional roles of department chairs, but the new edition offers important advice about how to respond to new roles associated with such current topics as assessment, accreditation, technology, and resource management.

While a conceptual understanding of the role of the chair is a necessary condition to lead, it is not sufficient without the mastery of appropriate behaviors and skills. In order to carry out their roles and responsibilities effectively, department chairs need to *develop their skills*. Fortunately, some of the requisite skills, such as communication, problem solving, and decision making, are transferable from other domains and can be quite easily built on within the context of academic leadership. Others, such as performance coaching, conflict resolution, negotiations, and resource management, may initially be less familiar to those who have little experience with supervision or administration. However, most of them can be developed through presentations, practice, and guided experience. The more multifaceted and complex skills associated with developing a strategic vision, building consensus, and inspiring confidence and trust require more time and generally greater assistance. The *Handbook* is particularly helpful in identifying the skills chairs need to survive, succeed, and even excel in leading largely self-directed professionals. The authors' advice is invariably sensible, measured, and sensitive to context. They advocate for strong and courageous leadership, but avoid simplifying or glossing over the realities of life in academic departments.

No less important than a *conceptual understanding* of the role of an academic leader and the acquisition of the *skills* necessary to achieve personal and departmental goals is the habit of *reflective practice*, which involves a kind of knowing-in-action. As the interviewees in the *Handbook* demonstrate so well, effective chairs often know more than they say and generally exhibit a form of tacit knowledge about their roles, aspirations, and strategies. Reflective practitioners are characteristically sensitive to their environment, curious, open-minded, and self-critical. In short, they are committed to learning from their experiences. The authors of the *Handbook* clearly believe in the efficacy of reflective practice and have included, as bookends to their chapters, questions to prompt thoughts while reading the chapters, as well as to reflect on ways that the material can be used afterward. In a similar vein, they provide a self-scored diagnostic questionnaire at the outset and a topical index of strategies at the conclusion, which encourage readers to reflect on their practices and to consider ways that other approaches might augment their current understanding of their roles and the skills required to succeed in them.

Thanks to the pioneering work of Allan Tucker, the authors of *The Academic Chairperson's Handbook*, and a host of others who have since contributed to our understanding of the critical function of academic leadership, we are less ignorant than we once were about the challenges individuals in these roles face and the skills and supports they need to be successful. Department chairs now have access to books, newsletters, listservs, conferences, and workshops to assist them in mastering their difficult roles. However, while much good work has been accomplished over the past two decades, much more remains to be done. The timely appearance of this substantially updated version of the *Handbook* serves to remind us of the challenges each successive generation of chairs encounters, as well as those challenges that are unique to this time and place in higher education. I welcome the reappearance of this highly accessible and relevant handbook.

Walter H. Gmelch
University of San Francisco
October 2007

Preface

*This book is addressed primarily to those who need to
know how university administration works, rather
than to those who want to know. That is, it is
intended more for practitioners than for scholars.*
—*Walker, 1986*

Background to the First Edition

There is more than a little truth to the old saying that "experience
is a hard teacher because she gives the test first, the lesson afterward." *The Academic Chairperson's Handbook* (Creswell, Wheeler,
Seagren, Egly, & Beyer, 1990) was originally conceived as a primer
to assist faculty in preparing for the myriad tests associated with
chairing an academic department. New chairs frequently enter their
positions with little preparation for the complexities of the role or
the challenges associated with it. They are often chosen on the basis
of their performance as scholars and teachers, or simply because it
is their turn, or no one else was willing to assume the responsibility. Many learn the job through painful trial and error. This *Handbook* aims to assist chairs in making a successful transition from
academic to administrative work. In the spirit of Walker's influential work on university administration, the *Handbook* was inten-
tionally designed to serve as a practical and accessible resource for
novice and experienced chairs alike.

The project initially grew out of a three-year, grant-funded study based on interviews with 200 department chairs on 70 campuses nationwide (see Appendix A). All the chairs were nominated by their institutions on the basis of their perceived effectiveness in providing strong leadership, supporting faculty development, and fostering a positive departmental climate. The interviews proved to be a rich source of hard-won experience and field-tested advice. By incorporating many of the interviewees' comments directly into the text, the authors were able to give voice to the personal aspirations and disappointments of these seasoned academic leaders.

Every attempt was made to preserve the original flavor and form of direct comments by department chairs. Their words reflected personal feelings of hope, frustration, anxiety, sadness, and surprise, as well as the regional colloquialisms of everyday speech. Their comments ultimately helped to inform the book's general strategies and specific applications. The book's framework was also influenced by perspectives drawn from human, organizational, and career development; from systems theory; and from the literature on interpersonal communications. The book drew heavily on recent research on faculty careers, faculty development, and academic leadership. The effectiveness of the unique voice and practical advice embodied in the first edition of the *Handbook* was validated subsequently by the hundreds of participants who attended workshops and seminars conducted for chairs, using the book as a major resource.

Focus of the Second Edition

Prior to embarking on a revision of the *Handbook*, the current authors surveyed both the literature and the landscape of higher education and returned to the field to conduct an additional 38 interviews on 24 campuses (see Appendix A). Our purpose was twofold: to substantiate the ongoing relevance of material contained in the original publication and to identify new issues and strategies that should be included in an updated version. Generally, what we discovered was sobering, if not altogether surprising, to those currently working in the field of higher education.

Our research confirmed, for example, that the day-to-day challenges associated with chairing academic departments have not so much changed as they have intensified. Personnel issues continue to consume considerable time and energy, but the number and nature of personal faculty issues have increased significantly. The steadily changing demographic profiles of institutions, including an aging professoriate and a growing reliance on adjunct faculty, have also added to the complexity of the chair's role. Similarly, student-related issues ranging from rising expectations and increasing consumerism to growing problems associated with academic dishonesty and changing learning habits are all having a profound effect on departmental operations. Scarce resources and the need to look for alternative funding sources are placing an additional burden on chairs as they struggle to deal with such issues as recruitment, research support, curriculum development, and the costs associated with technology implementation.

In addition to these day-to-day challenges, many observers have pointed out, and the department chairs we interviewed confirm, that one of the most dramatic developments in recent years has been the shift in public policy as it relates to higher education (Kerr, 2002; Massy, 1996; Tierney, 1998). In virtually every jurisdiction, institutions have had to adjust to external demands for greater efficiency, responsiveness, and accountability at the same time that they have experienced major reductions in their traditional sources of funding. Institutions are expected to consume fewer resources and produce more tangible results. Increasingly, higher education finds itself operating under market conditions where institutions must compete for scarce resources while meeting the demands of cost- and quality-conscious consumers (Chait, 2002; Pew Higher Education Roundtable, 1994). Higher education institutions are being required to demonstrate the quality of their product in relation to the investment made in them by funding agencies. In the process, they are having to shift their focus from traditional assets or inputs (endowments, library holdings, admission standards, etc.) to products or outcomes—what graduates have learned and what they are able to do with their learning.

It is against this backdrop that contemporary department chairs must go about the difficult task of addressing issues of access, affordability, quality, and accountability. Theirs is the challenge of providing effective leadership for their departments during a time of enormous change in higher education. What we discovered through our interviews is both how aware department chairs are of the major forces that are at play in their environment and how resourceful they are in devising practical strategies for dealing with the changing conditions within which faculty work and students learn. Revisions to the *Handbook* reflect many of these new realities and the techniques that current department chairs are employing to deal with them.

Plan of the Book

Readers who are familiar with the first edition of the *Handbook* will recognize that, while we have retained the general framework and much of the content of the original chapters, we have introduced a substantial amount of new material, including chapters on technology, funding and resources, departmental climate and quality, and assessment and accreditation. We have incorporated fresh quotes from interviewees, additional resources, and updated references. We have retained the earlier feature of posing questions and have added new questions to prompt reflection and further inquiry about the major topics. We believe that one of the most effective ways to move a department forward is by having the chair engage the faculty in a reflective process, asking questions in an open and trusting environment, and focusing on institutional mission and vision, faculty needs, and student expectations and demands.

The *Handbook* is divided into two sections. In Part I we describe several challenges department chairs encounter in building a positive work environment that fosters the professional growth and development of both faculty and chairs. A self-assessment inventory at the end of Chapter 1 is followed by three chapters outlining 15 strategies that chairs can employ to overcome common difficulties in the building process. These strategies are organized around themes of self-development, academic leadership, and interpersonal relationships.

In Part II we apply the strategies, first as a series of processes you might use to address specific departmental issues, and second as a general guide to building a positive and productive work environment. We suggest that you familiarize yourself with the strategies outlined in Part I first and that you choose to read the chapters in Part II according to your particular needs and interests at the time. You should be aware as you peruse the chapters that difficulties and their remedies are context specific and that, therefore, you should adapt advice in these chapters to suit your unique departmental circumstance. The strategies we present for your consideration might confirm established approaches or present you with alternative perspectives. Although the examples cited are from other departments and institutions than your own, examining ways you can adapt the strategies to your situation will provide you with a greater range of possible responses to issues as they arise within the context of your department.

The strategies are purposefully upbeat, positive, and developmental. Nevertheless, our presentation does not attempt to mask the sometimes harsh political realities involved in chairing academic departments. However, although the chairs we interviewed discussed their struggles and frustrations candidly, they did not dwell on the negative features of their jobs; they tended to deal with day-to-day setbacks in a resolute manner and maintained a positive long-range attitude. We conclude Part II with a chapter containing a general guide to the departmental building process, and we offer a series of steps for building your department. We provide additional information about the interviews conducted for both editions of the *Handbook* in Appendix A, and we provide a topical index to the strategies in Appendix B.

Audience

The principal audience for this *Handbook* is, of course, department chairs and heads of departments or similarly titled front-line administrative positions. The *Handbook* can serve as a helpful overview for prospective chairs, as a guide for new chairs, and as a resource for more experienced chairs. The text recognizes that not all chairs are appointed similarly and that not all chairs have identical responsibilities and authority. However, it assumes that all chairs are essentially *primus inter pares* and that they occupy that shadowy region between faculty and administration.

Others may also find the *Handbook* useful. Deans and other members of senior administration might gain insights into the workaday world of academic departments and the unique challenges facing their chairs. Faculty development personnel can look to the *Handbook* for ideas about workshops and in-service activities for faculty and chairs. Finally, faculty themselves can use the *Handbook* to gain a perspective and discover strategies that might improve on departmental operations that affect them directly.

Acknowledgements

The authors of this edition would like to acknowledge the generous support of the Lilly Endowment and TIAA-CREF, which made the research for the original publication possible. We are also appreciative of the efforts of the University of Nebraska Press in publishing the first edition. We would like to express our gratitude to the book's original authors, others who gave so freely of their advice, and the many individuals who assisted in the production of the manuscript. We would also like to thank the department chairs who were so forthright in sharing their experiences for the benefit of others.

The second edition of the *Handbook* would not have been possible were it not for the encouragement and support provided by Jim Anker. His belief in the value of the book as a beneficial practical resource for chairs spurred on the project. The staff at Anker Publishing were invariably helpful, and none more so than Carolyn Dumore, whose steady editorial hand improved our efforts at every turn. During the latter stages of this project, Jossey-Bass Publishers acquired Anker Publishing and guided this *Handbook* to publication. We are grateful to the editorial staff at Jossey-Bass for their careful assistance throughout the transition. Max Kirk and Helen Whippy were particularly helpful in designing the interview protocol and in conducting many of the interviews for the second edition of the *Handbook*. Cindy DeRyke at the University of Nebraska–Lincoln provided excellent administrative support. Walt Gmelch not only provided the Foreword to the book but gave generously of advice on many occasions. His own work on chairing academic departments has been an inspiration to all of us. Judy Eifert contributed wise advice based on her extensive experience as a chair, dean, and vice president. Her careful review of the manuscript was invaluable.

We thank all of those who have helped us in ways direct and indirect to produce this second edition. They have saved us from many mistakes along the way, but we absolve them of any responsibility for errors we might have persisted in.

Suggested Resources

Chait, R. (2002). The "academic revolution" revisited. In S. J. Brint (Ed.), *The future of the city of intellect: The changing American university* (pp. 294–391). Stanford, CA: Stanford University Press.

Chait's essay revisits Jencks and Riesman's classic 1960s celebration of the rise to power of the academic profession and examines the subsequent developments that have diluted the ideal and created much current disillusionment within the academy. Chait concludes that the issue is not as simple as the loss of power by faculty to administrators and boards but the incursion of market forces that have rendered all institutional players less powerful. This article is a useful primer for those wishing to understand how market forces are affecting institutional autonomy, roles, and decision making.

Kerr, C. (2002). Shock wave II: An introduction to the twenty-first century. In S. J. Brint (Ed.), *The future of the city of intellect: The changing American university* (pp. 1–19). Stanford, CA: Stanford University Press.

As an astute observer of trends in higher education, Kerr outlines the major features of Shock Wave I, which encompasses the development of

American higher education from its origins to the 1970s. Kerr believes that
we are now experiencing Shock Wave II, a far more rapid and discontinu-
ous set of changes than anything experienced previously. He identifies eight
key changes he believes will transform our institutions, and he proposes several strategies that might help us to cope with those massive forces.

Massy, W. F. (1996, Winter). New thinking on academic restructuring. *Priorities*,
6, 1–16.

Massy identifies the major long-term threats as public concerns about
the quality and relevance of undergraduate education, academic productivity, and the teaching–research balance. He encourages boards to support their institutions in shifting their focus from input to outcome
measures and to recognize that departments are the catalysts for fundamental curricular change.

Pew Higher Education Roundtable. (1994). To dance with change. *Policy Perspectives*, 5(3), 1–12.

The authors maintain that the changes most important to higher education are those that are external to it. "[Their] argument is simple and to
_the point: no institution will emerge unscathed from its confrontation
with an external environment that is substantially altered and in many
ways more hostile to colleges and universities" (p. 2). Their proposals for
change include making institutions more nimble, simplifying the curriculum, and encouraging collective action.

Tierney, W. G. (1998). On the road to recovery and renewal: Reinventing academe. In W. G. Tierney (Ed.), *The responsive university: Restructuring for
high performance* (pp. 1–12). Baltimore, MD: The Johns Hopkins University Press.

Acknowledging that techniques to improve what universities already
do can be useful, Tierney and his collaborators in this volume seek fundamentally new strategies to make universities more responsive to contemporary challenges and more adept at meeting the intellectual, economic,
and social demands being placed on them.

Walker, D. E. (1986). *The effective administrator: A practical approach to problem solving, decision making, and campus leadership*. San Francisco, CA: Jossey-Bass.

Originally published in 1979, this practical guide to academic leadership has retained its freshness and relevance. Walker operates within a
political "frame" but is also highly sensitive to other frames of reference,
including human relations, structural, and symbolic. Engaging and infor-
mative, the book contains helpful advice from a seasoned practitioner.
Readers might also find the author's axioms of considerable use as well.

Part I

Fifteen Strategies in the Building Process

1

Difficulties in the Building Process

If one can create a sense of community, which allows
for individual and collective programs, personal devel-
opment, and a sense of family to celebrate personal
and collective accomplishments, a department can be
a wonderful and enjoyable place to work. However,
without a sense of community and family a depart-
ment can be a terrible place to work in terms of hav-
ing fun, being productive, and gaining satisfaction.
—A chair of a large humanities department

Creating and maintaining a positive work environment for faculty is a goal to which most chairs aspire, and which can be
characterized in several ways. Ideally, faculty feel they are appreciated and supported, and in turn, they feel a commitment to the
department. They support and embrace the department's mission
and are aligned with its goals and objectives. They also believe that
their individual goals and objectives are appreciated and respected.
While this might appear to be a somewhat utopian view, it does represent a vision of what departments can at least work toward, if not
completely attain.

The Context for Leadership

The environment within which chairs operate today is vastly more complex and multidimensional than the one inhabited by their predecessors only a few years ago.

> Higher education, facing change and high risks, is in need of new and better leadership now—not just in the presidency but at all levels. Leadership is not something that should be hoarded; it is not a zero-sum game. The goal must be to expand the number of leaders and the total amount of leadership. This means that institutions must make a continuous effort in two critical areas. The first is to improve the search process. The second is the need for leadership development—a subject that is not addressed at all on most campuses, leaving higher education as one of the few sectors of society that does not focus on a constant effort to find and develop leaders. (Newman, Couturier, & Scurry, 2004, p. 198)

Chairs today might feel at times that they are performing in a drama where not everyone is working from the same script; where actors come and go seemingly randomly; where members of the audience participate spontaneously in the action itself from time to time; and where critics who might never have seen an actual performance nevertheless pass judgment on its quality.

In periods of rapid and momentous change, such as higher education is currently experiencing, it is very challenging to get all the players in a department, far less in an entire institution, on the same page, so to speak. Compounding this problem is the fact that faculty lead very busy lives and often have only limited and intermittent attention to devote to departmental and institutional priorities. In addition, formerly passive spectators—students, parents, and the general public—have begun to get far more involved in the process and outcomes of higher education. Finally, regulatory authorities and policymakers have become much more vocal about what they consider to be the inadequacies of higher education. In short, these are some of the more vocal players who might at times operate from scripts that are quite different from those commonly found in colleges and universities.

Figure 1.1 conveys the dramatic interplay of forces that affect chairs and their departments. At the core of the enterprise lies learning and performance, which carry connotations of outcomes and productivity, two watchwords that are associated with the current educational environment. Surrounding these core functions of higher education are the systems, processes, and practices that departments employ—and chairs lead—to ensure that they produce the desired results. Building on a base of mutual trust, departments open themselves to collaboration and teamwork that lead to deeper understandings of what they do and how they do it. Ultimately, understanding forms the basis for improvement and assessment. In a fully functioning department where all of these preconditions are met, chairs can work with their faculty to envision a positive future and put realizable plans in place to ensure that common goals are achieved.

Creating a positive and productive departmental culture is at once an enormous challenge for chairs and, if done properly, a source of deep satisfaction. While there are many factors that influence a work unit's culture, we identify a set of key elements, including change management, quality assurance, assessment and accountability, advice and support, and effective leadership. How chairs work with their faculty to create conditions where innovation, quality, and results are embraced as goals for the entire department determines the extent to which they will enjoy a positive climate. We will have much more to say about these elements of departmental culture in the chapters that follow.

At yet another level, chairs participate in and are influenced by their institution's governance structures. This is not only the level at which comprehensive policies and priorities are established, but it is the buffer between the institution and its various external stakeholders. Given the rise in activity levels in the external environment, which we referred to in the Preface, the governance system in insti-

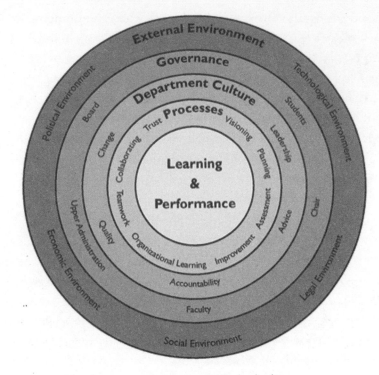

FIGURE 1.1.   The department chair's context for leadership.

tutions has also become more active in engaging public bodies that
have an interest in their operations. Once a sanctuary for the unfet-
tered creation and expression of ideas and opinions, colleges and universities have been opened up to the play of competitive market
forces and the scrutiny of policymakers and the general public.

Finally, what we call the external environment consists of a con-
stellation of active forces that impinge on institutional autonomy and
self-regulation. They include elected officials who respond to the public's demand for greater efficiency and accountability; sharp reductions in public subsidies to higher education; changing demographics
and access issues; an increasingly litigious environment; and the proliferation and convergence of information technologies. However, it
would be shortsighted to simply view the relationship between institutions and their environment as one in which institutions are passive while the environment is active. More and more institutions are

engaging in competitive and collaborative activities ranging from establishing campuses abroad to creating spin-off companies.

This chapter presents three realities that chairs face in building a positive culture and climate: aspects related to chairing a department; characteristics of academic departments; and pressing problems facing faculty. The chapter ends with a self-assessment inventory that serves both as a means for chairs and faculty to identify concerns, as well as a way to direct attention to relevant sections of the book for suggestions or ideas.

Chairing the Department

Chairs are busy people. Daily, they face tough decisions about recruiting, developing and evaluating faculty, providing raises, managing conflicts, mediating tensions, and counseling faculty about diverse topics such as promotion and tenure, midlife crises, personal and professional growth, and retirement. These responsibilities suggest myriad roles and tasks, well-documented in the literature on chairing academic departments.[1] Implicit within these roles and tasks are the dual responsibilities of loyalty and support to the institution and advocacy for staff in the department. A continual need exists to resolve tensions on both these horizontal and vertical levels (Brown, 1977).

Individuals assume the position of chair at substantial cost to their professional interests and scholarly careers. Chairs have difficulty maintaining active lives as faculty and scholars. Moreover, the financial compensation is not commensurate with the time and energy required to perform chair duties. A chair's length of appointment seldom extends beyond two three-year or one five-year term, thereby causing institutions to underutilize individuals with administrative talents and create discontinuity in departmental leadership. This short-term prospect also means that individuals must give serious consideration to what to do after being a chair. Training for new chairs in administration and leadership often takes the form of on-the-job experience or observation of admired leaders. Like other academic administrators on campuses, departmental leaders do what they have either observed others do when they were in these roles or emulate, often incorrectly, some other figures of the past, fantasies of Harvard Business School products, General Patton, creatures of fiction or movies, or some atavisms of leadership and authority which never were. (Bennis, 1973, p. 397)

Chairpersons are appointed by administrators, elected by faculty, or some combination of these methods for offices to which they might neither aspire nor actively seek. Eble (1986), a former English department chair and perceptive observer of academic departments, once observed:

Those who want the position are often ruled out for their wanting it. Those who don't want it are often and unwisely forced into it. Those who assume the position must face a disdain for administration from many of their colleagues and even from themselves. (p. 2)

Their busy lives as chairs and their lack of training often preclude investing substantial time in assisting faculty in their development. Reflection on your own career will help you recognize that other professionals played a significant role in your development. Thus, the journey toward helping others begins with an assessment of your own career. Further suggestions for considering your own development are provided in Chapter 2.

The Nature of the Department

Over the years supporters and critics have argued about the merits of academic departments on college campuses. Advocating for strong departmental leadership, Leaming (2007) addresses the present-day saliency of departments:

The bottom line is that the department remains the nexus of the university. If we are to solve problems, chairpersons must pave the way. They must help find research dollars, see that faculty remain current in knowledge and skills, get faculty to work collaboratively, and encourage faculty and students to embrace and acknowledge—with confidence and wisdom—that today's warp-speed changes demand urgent responses and adjustments. (p. xvi)

Despite these advantages for both chairs and faculty, the nature of academic departments creates difficulties for establishing a positive faculty work environment. Departments can inhibit the development of new fields of knowledge, contribute to the isolation of professors, and promote unnecessarily narrow specialization of courses and research (Andersen, 1977). These factors cause chairs difficulty in building faculty support for departmental goals and directions. Individuals can become advocates for their own narrow specializations, and their individual excellence does not necessarily equal excellence of the team. The culture of working together needs to be present if the department is to achieve its collective goals.

Faculty can withdraw into themselves and become isolated, which causes departmental strength and vitality to wax and wane. In such situations, academic departments do not become dynamic units where growth and development can occur. Chairs find it easier and more convenient in these instances to deflect this responsibility to faculty development centers, faculty committees, and academic deans. However, chairs should consider how they can capitalize on the strengths of departments in promoting a positive work environment for faculty and use other resources on and off campus to meet individual and departmental needs. Chapter 4 offers suggestions for creating a positive interpersonal work environment.

The Nature of Faculty Work

Interaction between chairs and faculty is a source of both satisfaction and frustration. Faculty want autonomy, but they request assistance; demand quick decisions yet belabor issues; seek power and authority but delegate decisions to administrators. Years of academic freedom have bred a workforce of rugged individualists who embrace peer group arrangements often described by terms such as *collegial*, *oligarchic*, *feudal*, or *caste-based* (Wolvoord, et al., 2000). Such arrangements or even perceptions of how departments should operate can create major issues in making changes, particularly those not initiated by the faculty. National reports about professors portray a changing picture of academic life marked by greater measures of accountability, fewer tenure-track positions, and less discretionary time to spend on preferred research and teaching activities. Evidence indicates that in recent years faculty work conditions have changed and even deteriorated on many campuses. Various reports also suggest that salaries are not keeping pace and faculty are expected to generate more resources for their institutions. Some would say that higher education is becoming more like a business through adopting many of the same procedures and tools, some of which might be appropriate for higher education, while others might not be appropriate at all to the context. All of these conditions suggest that even though faculty positions might still be seen as highly regarded, they require a different mindset and set of skills than in previous times.

A need exists for each chairperson to have a better understanding of the situation of their faculty with an eye toward means, both subtle and direct, that will facilitate good interpersonal communication with their staff and enable faculty to grow and develop.

A Self-Assessment

Before proceeding to other parts of this book, we suggest that readers complete the self-assessment checklist below. If you are a faculty member, consider whether the questions apply to your chairperson and department. Similarly, if you are a dean, consider the extent to which the questions are relevant to particular chairs you work with.

The list is not meant to exhaust all possible situations. It focuses on key issues or concerns identified by chairs in our study and directs the reader to specific portions of the book that might be helpful. After completing the assessment and reviewing strategies mentioned in the following chapters, try a few of them. Later, return to Chapter 13 of the book and review whether you have followed the dimensions of the building process.

The Building Process (Part I)

Answer each of the following with a yes or a no.

About the Self-Development of Chairs (Chapter 2)
1. Are your mentoring activities effective with faculty?
2. Have effective team relationships developed in the department?
3. Do you provide encouragement or reinforcement to faculty?
4. Do senior and new faculty work well together?
5. Do you have adequate knowledge about the department— its history, strengths, mission, faculty, and students—to be effective?
6. Have you built networks with other chairs and administrators on campus?
7. Have you achieved a balance among professional, personal, and leisure activities?
8. Do you have a plan for your career after serving as the chair?
9. Have you been able to keep current in your discipline or academic field?

About Leading an Academic Department (Chapter 3)
10. Has your department developed a clear vision for the future?
11. Do the faculty demonstrate ownership of and commitment to this vision?
12. Do you have an ongoing process to identify areas that are in need of change?
13. Is the process for the allocation of resources clearly understood by the faculty within the department?
14. Is the department database adequate to provide the information you need to make decisions?
15. Do faculty understand how data or information is used in decision making?

About Interacting Positively with Faculty (Chapter 4)

16. Do faculty in the department perceive that there is an open, supportive atmosphere or culture?
17. Are your listening skills effective?
18. Do you regularly assist faculty in setting realistic goals and priorities?
19. Do you provide regular feedback to faculty about their performance in the areas of teaching, research, scholarship, and service?
20. Are faculty aware of your role as an advocate for them with senior administration?
21. Do faculty perceive that you follow through on initiatives?

About Applying the Strategies to Specific Faculty Issues (Part II)

22. Do you have new faculty in your department who need to be oriented and acclimated to the unit? (Chapter 5)
23. Do senior faculty perceive that they have a role to play in developing new faculty? (Chapter 5)
24. Have you found ways to improve the teaching performance of faculty? (Chapter 6)
25. Do you need to improve the scholarly performance of faculty in your department? (Chapter 7)
26. Do you have faculty in the department who lack vitality and enthusiasm? (Chapter 8)
27. Is the performance of any faculty member being affected by personal problems? (Chapter 9)
28. Does your department have a technology plan, and is it used to inform curricular and budget decisions? (Chapter 10)
29. Is technology being used effectively as a teaching/learning tool? (Chapter 10)
30. Do faculty use technology effectively? (Chapter 10)
31. Do faculty understand the implications of reduced funding, and are they prepared to reallocate resources or seek new sources? (Chapter 11)

32. Are faculty willing to be entrepreneurial and look for new ways to deliver instruction? (Chapter 11)

33. Have you developed an agenda with your faculty that will support and strengthen your department as it changes over time? (Chapter 12)

34. Are faculty committed to quality and productivity in teaching, research, and service? (Chapter 12)

If you have answered several of these questions with "yes," give yourself and your faculty a pat on the back. For those you answered with "no," or if you found yourself saying, "sometimes," "we used to," "some of us," or "I wish," then you will find the chapters that follow beneficial to you as an academic leader as you develop strategies, activities, and processes designed to change or inspire your department.

Endnotes

1. For a comprehensive identification of chairperson roles, readers should consult Seagren, Creswell, and Wheeler (1993). For a discussion of the four roles of a chairperson—leader, manager, developer, and scholar—readers should consult Gmelch and Miskin (2004).

Suggested Resources

Andersen, K. J. (1977). In defense of departments. In D. E. McHenry & Associates, *Academic departments: Problems, variations, and alternatives* (pp. 1–12). San Francisco, CA: Jossey-Bass.

   Andersen's chapter begins by tracing the history of the academic department back to Harvard University in 1739, then she describes the evolution of departments and the influence of the early universities in Europe and England. She quotes famous people, such as Thomas Jefferson, who strongly supported the importance of an academic department to the educational process. The article also includes sections that describe critics of departments and the advantages of departments, and it concludes with some strategies for improving departments.

Brown, J. D. (1977). Departmental and university leadership. In D. E. McHenry & Associates, *Academic departments: Problems, variations, and alternatives* (pp. 189–205). San Francisco, CA: Jossey-Bass.

Brown's chapter emphasizes the importance of academic freedom in the organization of universities. He then describes the importance of departmental leadership and expectations. This leadership must acknowledge the nature of faculty and the role of committees. The chapter concludes with a discussion of the role of the dean and president in relationship to departmental leadership.

Leaming, D. R. (2007). *Academic leadership: A practical guide to chairing the department* (2nd ed.). Bolton, MA: Anker.

The author, a former department chair and dean, provides a guide to the overall management of the department. Along with much sage advice, Leaming provides ideas and strategies to address the multitude of departmental and institutional processes involving personnel and everyday matters that are crucial to effectiveness. He provides illustrations and methods to address salient issues. Many helpful references are identified.

Seagren, A. T., Creswell, J. W., & Wheeler, D. W. (1993). *The department chair: New roles, responsibilities, and challenges*. Washington, DC: The George Washington University, Graduate School of Education and Human Development.

This monograph reviews the research on department chairing and emphasizes strategies for effectiveness. Areas addressed include roles and responsibilities, chair as leader, chair's politics and power, role in faculty evaluation and development, influence of academic disciplines, and future challenges.

Wolvoord, B. E., Carey, A. K., Smith, H. L., Soled, S. W., Way, P. K., & Zorn, D. (2000). *Academic departments: How they work, how they change* (ASHE-ERIC Higher Education Report, Vol. 27, No. 8). Washington, DC: The George Washington University, Graduate School of Education and Human Development.

This publication provides an overview of departments and makes the case for why and how they can make changes. The focus is not only on what departments look like today but how they need to be. Beyond a case made for both external and internal pressures for change, many ideas are presented for how departments can make changes. The book explores the research behind academic values, disciplines, relations with central administration, departmental organization, departmental leadership, and departmental work with implications for change. Numerous examples and research findings are provided to reinforce the change emphasis. An extensive bibliography is included.

2

Consider Your Own Development

Without some self-development, chairs cannot be energized to work with faculty.
— *A chair of a social sciences department*

A prerequisite for encouraging the professional growth of faculty is commitment to your own growth. Assuming the position of department chair is not the end but, rather, the beginning of a developmental journey that is focused on leadership, personal development, and organizational change. This means seeing yourself as part of a dynamic process in which you are changing, maturing, looking for new insights, and reflecting on patterns of thought and behavior. It also means seeing yourself as learning and gaining from interactions with faculty and other administrators who can be invaluable in assisting you in the design and implementation of a personal development plan. You must move beyond yourself and into the perceptual world of others. As writers in counseling and related fields recommend, to facilitate the careers of others you need to "know yourself" (Brammer, 1979).

With the opportunities for 360-degree feedback and other sophisticated feedback procedures, chairs can gain considerable insight into and perspective on their roles and lives. There are several instruments and applications that can be used in the process of a 360-degree view. Some of the more common ones are:

- MLQ (Multifactor Leadership Questionnaire)
- DiSC (Personal Profile System)
- MBTI (Myers-Briggs Type Indicator)
- StrengthsQuest (Gallup)[1]

None of these instruments provide information that tells a chair what to do or when to do it, but they are all helpful in the process of reflective practice in relation to questions such as:

- How do I see myself, how do my subordinates see me, and how do my superiors see me?
- Am I perceived in the way I want to be?
- What sorts of changes in behavior should I consider?
- Does a positive work environment exist?
- How should my development plan reflect the changes I want to make?

If the responses to these questions result in conflicting points of view, these perspectives may provide you with an excellent opportunity to analyze and then discuss these divergent views with others in an effort to understand and respond appropriately.

None of these instruments are an end in themselves nor do they paint a perfect picture of the situation. Rather, each is simply a reflection of perceptions. Some chairs might want to use more than one instrument. It is not just collecting the information about the perceptions that is important, however, but it is how the collected information is used that makes a difference. Some chairs have found that the use of these instruments can be helpful not only for providing ideas for self-development but also for departmental development. They can be useful in analyzing areas of concern or issues that need to be addressed or where modifications might be made. Modeling the use of these types of instruments can be an effective way to get a department to engage in a continuous process of reflection and change. Engaging in a process of appreciative inquiry,[2] as suggested in the types of questions posed above, can go a long way toward creating a culture that is open to change.

The first step in considering your own development is to take a reading on how you stack up on several dimensions from multiple perspectives. As a chair you have leadership responsibilities that cause you to ask a set of questions that are quite different from those you asked when you were a faculty member. As a faculty member you tended to ask, "How can I be more effective as a teacher to help students learn and develop, contribute to my discipline through research, and provide service to the department, college, university, and larger community?" Now, as the chair, the questions are more likely to be, "How will my behavior as a leader help faculty be more productive; how can we be more effective in providing the curriculum and instructional strategies that will assist and prepare students for the future; and how can I create a culture of change, quality, and people development?" Fundamentally, you want to know, "How will the department, college, and institution be better because of what I do as chair?"

A second step in your self-development is to ask yourself the question, "Why and how was I selected to be the chair?" How the stage was set or how or why you became chair can have a huge impact on what you consider in your plans for your own self-development.

As a chair-apparent you need to know the answers to several critical questions: Who are you following in the chair position? A long-term chair or a short-term chair? Was she or he well liked and respected? What kind of a department was the chair presiding over? Contentious? Productive? Stale? Why is the chair leaving? A need for new blood? A better opportunity? Mismanagement? Lack of leadership? Tired administrator? Administrative conflicts with those above? For example, if you are following a well-liked, respected, productive chair, meeting those established standards might be difficult, especially at first. On the other hand, if you are following a chair with poor relations, with a lack of success, or with ineffective management skills, anything might seem better because the expectations are so low.

If you lack firsthand knowledge of your predecessor's performance or your department's productivity, engage in some reconnaissance work. Ask people with an informed perspective on the department to share their views. Read reports, minutes, and correspondence to gain impressions about how administrative business was conducted. Thoughtful analysis and strategy can help to set realistic expectations and prevent early difficulties.

This chapter provides an opportunity for you to explore your own professional life. We discuss three strategies for chair self-development based on the observations of exemplary chairs. These are intended to help faculty relate professional goals to departmental and institutional goals and missions, and for you to learn about your role and responsibilities as chair. To be fresh, alert, and rested to help another person requires that you balance your personal and professional lives. To assist individual faculty members in planning their careers, you should review your own long-range career plans.

Reflect on these three questions as you read this chapter:

- How did you learn about the departmental and institutional contexts in which they work?
- How did you balance their personal and professional lives?
- How did you plan for their own careers as administrators or faculty?

Learn About Your Role and Responsibilities in the Department and the Institution

Wolvoord and colleagues (2000) provide a thoughtful context for considering the history and possibilities in the department:

> Departments at their best are the flexible belt, not the fixed cog, that translates intellectual energy into multiple kinds of services to multiple constituencies. Departments are deeply influenced by their disciplines and are guided by powerful traditional values, including collegiality and autonomy. Some evidence suggests that collegial models are most successful; however, current

> demands from stakeholders ask departments to change in just those ways that traditional collegiality is least able to address. . . . We view departments not as fossils but as living organisms struggling to construct new forms in the face of these challenges, to be more outwardly oriented, more innovative, and more entrepreneurial, to emphasize results, to collaborate more closely with a wide variety of disciplines and external agencies, and to reward effectively all types of faculty for their achievements. (p. 85)

Certainly this suggests that the challenges related to the chair's role will be multifaceted and complex. It also assumes that these challenges are quite situational and depend on various environmental factors, as well as specific cultural features of departments.

Learning about the department will be easier if a chair has been a faculty member prior to assuming the new position. The ideal circumstance is to be groomed for the position over an extended period of time. A chair of an education department at a comprehensive university described an "internship" arrangement for in-house aspirants to the chair's position: "In our department faculty usually know three years ahead that they will assume the position. During these three years, they've been included in budgeting, accreditation, professional conferences for chairs, and aspects of decision making."

Especially important for a new chair or an individual coming to the department from the outside is the "advance preparation" needed to understand the department and its faculty. A chair in a forestry department commented:

> Take enough time to become truly familiar with the department, its faculty, programs, research thrusts, strengths, and weaknesses. I know that may be a luxury and may require a great deal of effort, but try to find time. Those first few months can be terribly stressful. Advance preparation can help.

This advance preparation is important. Few chairs are given an orientation when they assume their position. Gmelch (2006) captures the essence of the stress that new chairs experience:

> Chairs typically begin their positions without leadership training, without a clear understanding of the time demands involved, without knowing the conflict inherent in the position, and without an awareness of the stress and demands on their academic careers and personal lives. Many chairs love to help students and serve their colleagues—that is why they *are* chairs—but after they have experienced the frenzy and conflicting demands of the position, department chairs tend to return to the faculty after serving a single term.[3]

How does one prepare in advance? Consider visiting the department frequently and learn as much as possible about it before accepting the position. Analyze and study minutes of past departmental meetings, official institutional policies, and budget documents for the last few years. Review publications by faculty and examine student evaluations of teaching. Peruse program reviews or accreditation reports of the department. Read long-range planning documents and mission statements. Visit with faculty members and constituents to explore their general needs, interests, and perceptions of issues and problems facing the department. Also study institutional policies, planning documents, and whatever else is available in the external environment.

Learning about the department also involves understanding your responsibilities and knowing when matters should be delegated to others. Chairs are called on to solve many types of problems. March (1980), a nationally known authority on organizations, once said that what distinguishes a good bureaucracy from a bad one is "how well it accomplishes the trivia of day-to-day relations with clients and day-to-day problems in maintaining and operating its technology" (p. 17). Though department chairs might not characterize their units as bureaucracies, they would readily admit that they spend much time on minor day-to-day issues and problems. Before spending an inordinate amount of time on an issue, chairs might ask themselves, "Is this a problem I need to undertake, or should it be delegated to someone else?" As one individual commented, "You have to learn how to delegate authority, and you also have to learn what you are responsible for." In larger units, responsibilities can be delegated to vice chairs or assistant chairs. In smaller units, the range of issues can be extensive, as a biological sciences chair in a small liberal arts college pointed out:

> If the bathrooms are not clean, who else is there to tell but the chair? If there is a problem in the department, the chair has to accept the fact that she or he will become the sounding board for the problems. If the faculty are unhappy about something, the inclination is to tell the chair. You have to handle that and not be put off by it.

Learning about the department and the responsibility of chairing can be enhanced by visiting with experienced chairs who have solid reputations for success on campus and expertise in specific aspects of the job. The following observations came from individuals who were both new to the chair post as well as more experienced:

> I recommend that people new to the position visit with other chairs. Seek out individuals who have been in the position and who have learned how things work in the institution. As you become more savvy about the political process, the budget, and the management processes involved in the institution, you become more effective. (A new chair in psychology with two years of experience)

> I really would have drowned here the first month if I didn't share a secretary with an individual who had been here for 20 years and who, in my mind, had been a

superb chair for many of those years. The advice helped me to get my feet on the ground and to develop perspective. (A new chair in social sciences with three years of experience)

The chairs in our study suggested seeking out individuals with a reputation for having expertise in specific aspects of chairing:

Accept for one moment that you are not an administrative whiz kid, even if you think you are. Find the outstanding chairs at your institution and learn how they conduct evaluations. I can't emphasize enough how damaging a misspoken adjective can be on an evaluation or how productive a good evaluation can be. (A chair in medical sciences with eight years of experience)

In addition to informal visits with experienced individuals, you might benefit from a formal workshop on or off campus. One chair described a regular event on his campus:

The chairs of the departments meet to discuss important issues every month or six weeks. Some of the issues revolve around administrative responsibilities of the chairs. Recognizing variation in responsibilities and in function due to the nature, history, and discipline of the units, we discuss a wide range of approaches.

Aside from other chairs, senior administrators such as deans and campus-wide officials can be helpful. A mathematics chair of a regional university remarked somewhat facetiously: "Make sure you have a good dean to work with." Unfortunately, the selection of the dean is normally out of the chair's hands. Nonetheless, explore the nature of administrative support for your unit and the management styles of other administrators. Learn these through formal experiences at work and through social and informal means.

It is crucial that you "make sure the university hierarchy is committed to your program and goals and convince them through performance and creative programs that you have the single most dynamic program on campus," said a major research university chair in communications. Study the management styles of senior administrators. Learn the strengths and weaknesses of people who make decisions affecting the department:

> The squeaky wheel gets the grease. The chair needs to learn how to "squeak" in a diplomatic way. There will be a pay-off if the approach is appropriate. (A health–physical education and recreation chair at a regional doctoral-granting school)

> It's important for a chair to get to know the people who have some control over resources and who actually make decisions. Get to know the central administrators—the vice presidents and the president—where they're coming from, what they think, and what their motives are. This knowledge means more than becoming "acquainted" with them. (A philosophy chair at a state college)

How does an individual become more than "acquainted" with senior administrators? Interact with them on projects and campus-based activities. An anthropology chair at a state college recommended attending social gatherings:

> I would definitely recommend that the chair go to parties and receptions. Enhance visibility; meet people outside of your discipline with whom you interact. It is tremendously important to see, for instance, that there are two sides to the vice president of the budget; one is when you are dealing with formal budget requests, the other is when you see the person at a social gathering.

Through these approaches, you enhance opportunities for departmental support. As one individual said: "If they throw money at you, you know things are okay." Responding to external forces and expectations can also provide new opportunities for departmental programs and services.

In this period of high accountability, you need to be aware of and conduct an external environmental scan using the SWOT or STEP process to assess the impact of technology, legal, economic, and political forces on the department.

Create a Balance Between Your Professional and Personal Lives

Given the increasing demands on chairs to improve the performance and productivity of their departments, there is a tendency for the urgent (i.e., the crisis of the moment) to trump the important (i.e., personal health and stability). Hecht (2006) makes the point this way:

> There are so many people in the life of the chair that there is a risk of neglecting those who are personally important. Time needs to be reserved for them, whether it is time to help a child with homework or time to spend with the significant other in your life. It is easy to think that what you are doing is so important that you fail to take vacations even when the academic calendar permits you to do so. Not only should you take appropriate vacations, but it is also vital to set aside personal time when you are "present off the job." (p. 14)

A wise person once remarked that it is impossible to be happy in only one aspect of life. Individuals in our study advised fellow chairs to balance personal time—time with family, friends, and significant others—with department time. A medical chair at a major research university talked about setting aside time for family:

> Look out for yourself. I'm amazed how many people assume chair responsibilities and then their personal lives fall apart with divorce or other problems. Chairs

must take time to look out for their family relationships. They just can't drop it all. They shouldn't let the job overwhelm and inundate their personal time. They've got to say, "Okay, enough's enough. I'm spending the weekend with my family, and I'm not going to let anything interfere—barring a major emergency."

Note the escape clause in the final phrase. Chairs could classify all departmental issues as major emergencies: That faculty member's request can't wait until Monday! I must get the memos out! The budget must be completed over the weekend or we will not receive the grant! Exemplary chairs in our study recommended exercising considerable restraint in classifying issues as major emergencies.

The importance of a commitment to family and the strength that can be derived from such an orientation were emphasized by two chairs. A relatively new chair in a small liberal arts institution said:

> I think it works well to set aside specific time for personal needs. Families don't automatically have to suffer when an individual assumes the chair. I know a lot of colleagues whose good marriages fell apart when they became chair. I'm sure chairs are well above the national average in the divorce rate. I have four children. Although I wouldn't give myself accolades, I think I have held my family commitment together pretty well.

"It is easy to get caught in the trap of overemphasizing the importance of the department," said a veteran chair of a social sciences department with five years of experience. He went on to provide the following cautionary advice:

> Some chairs let their families go. They get enough ego boost from their job that they let their families fall apart. Still, they keep on working and it doesn't bother them. But it can be devastating in the long run. I think my

family actually allows me to do a better job. I'm fresher, more alert, and have a better attitude if I'm not inundated with my department for 99 hours a week, 52 weeks of the year.

Personal time can be increased by using common sense methods for being more efficient at the job. Chairs handle considerable paperwork and small chores sometimes called "administrivia." Reports must be prepared, memos written, inquiries answered, telephone calls returned, emails responded to, students registered, budgets developed, and class schedules organized. You can profit from time-saving techniques. "Get petty, necessary things done quickly so you can concentrate on the important things," commented one chair. Others had more specific solutions: "Get an answering machine to help reduce the amount of time consumed or utilized on the telephone," or "Develop the ability to deal with a lot of little things all at once," or "Become a 'list maker,' an 'organizer,' a 'facilitator.' Grease the wheel so things will work that aren't necessarily working." Other chairs recommended similar approaches for handling paperwork:

> Don't get bogged down in paperwork. Make sure you can see the big picture—where the department is going and what the faculty needs. If you can't figure out how to get paperwork off your desk, delegate someone else to handle it. (A chair of a plant sciences department)

> I don't like paperwork. I try to do it as quickly as possible so I have it around for a minimal period of time. (A chair of a chemical engineering department)

> Concentrate on making sure the paper flows. (A chair of a social sciences department)

The frequency with which chairs volunteered advice about managing time efficiently on administrative tasks speaks to how important they consider these skills to be, not just for efficiency but also for sheer survival. In our experience, effective chairs are well organized, keep the paperwork flowing, use time-saving methods in their jobs, and reserve time for themselves and their families.

With present-day technology, achieving balance takes on new challenges and meaning. On the one hand, chairs can be accessed 24/7, making it apparent that they are aware of and expected to respond to issues in real time, so to speak. On the other hand, getting away might require leaving the laptop at the office or having an arrangement that there will only be contact in an emergency. Without question, technology has made some things easier, but it must be managed to prevent the possibility of chairs being overwhelmed. We devote Chapter 10 to issues related to employing technology wisely for your benefit as well as the department's. Some questions your might ask yourself about your attitude toward accessibility are:

- What does it mean to be accessible?
- How often will you check email? Twice a day? More? What times?
- How can you use technology to increase your effectiveness? Efficiency?
- How do you model balance? Why is it important for you and the department?

Another aspect of balance is to set aside time for activities that provide personal time. Physical exercise, for example, can provide a mental break in your routine and contribute to a fresh and alert mind. A chair at a liberal arts college had the following advice about fitness:

> Try to keep yourself physically fit. I think you have to set aside certain times for exercise. Go bicycling at 9:00 a.m. or to the university recreation facilities and work out from 3:00 to 4:00 p.m. Ask your secretary to map time out on your calendar, especially when you have heavily scheduled weeks and when you know you need a mental break.

Often inexperienced chairs fear that they will be chastised by faculty for their exercise breaks. One chair disagreed with this assessment:

> I've never gotten flack from the faculty and the department for taking time off for physical activity. If anything, faculty respect me for keeping myself in good physical condition. I think I'm more physically and mentally alert because of it. I'm not talking about people who put 30 hours a week into fitness. I'm talking about an honest 3 hours a week, half of which conflicts with the time I'm expected to be in the office. Too many young chairs get started and then just fall apart with high blood pressure or family problems.

This individual not only gained faculty respect for time away from the office, he also benefited from being more alert because of his physical regimen. Chairs have an important role to play in modeling the type of behavior they wish to encourage in others. Model unhealthy devotion to work and you will attract some followers but also many who resent your unrealistic work ethic.

Prepare for Your Professional Future

It is relatively easy to slip into an administrative role, get caught up in the hectic pace of the job, and not consider where, ultimately, the experience is leading. Reflective chairs stop to ask themselves a series of searching questions at intervals along the way. "Do I plan to return to a primary professional career as a faculty member or researcher or become involved in administrative activities on a permanent basis?" "What activities give me the greatest satisfaction— leadership and management or scholarly activities such as teaching, research, and service?" "What will I do after I have completed my tenure as chair?" These questions remind us of the 14th lesson advanced some years ago by Kimble in his work *A Departmental*

Chairperson's Survival Manual (1979): "Prepare for your own demise as chairman" (p. 4). Assessing and planning for the future represents an integral part of a chair's self-development. An earth sciences chair at a doctoral-granting school emphasized the need to carefully examine and assess options rather than simply have events overtake you:

> If you want to assume a chairmanship, do a soul search. Determine whether your career plans are to remain a faculty member or a researcher or to move up administratively. In some of the hard sciences like biology, for example, a chairmanship can very often ruin a research career. However, if the person wants to move up administratively, the chair position would be a good step.

Though the chair position might place your teaching and research activities on hold or severely limit the time devoted to them, it also opens opportunities for an administrative career. Whether you intend to pursue administration or decide to return to the faculty later, assessing your long-range professional goals helps maintain appropriate professional priorities during your term in office.

Chairs we interviewed cautioned repeatedly that unless this soul search is done, actually serving in the position can significantly jeopardize an academic career. For example, a chair of a social science department at a research university observed:

> The chair position should not be a dead end. I've known several chairs who didn't have anywhere to go after their terms. They didn't move up in administration; maybe they didn't want to. But they hadn't sufficiently planned ahead for their own careers.

Chairs who eventually plan to return to full-time teaching or research after their service as chairs can enhance a successful return by maintaining an intellectual focus in their discipline or field of study or by retooling before resuming a faculty post. A department chair in social sciences at a research university said, "Maintain your stature as a scholar. Be concerned with your own professional activities." Although this might be especially true for people in research institutions, a chair at a liberal arts college made a similar comment: "I would advise chairs that keeping themselves intellectually alive is the most important thing for their overall growth and development. Chairs must be involved in some challenging intellectual focus in both teaching and in their field."

A chair of a social sciences department at a research university alluded to the importance of taking time to sharpen one's saw from time to time:

> A chair has to pay a lot of attention to how she develops as a scholar. Pay attention to the edge and notice if the edge is getting dull. The chair is a service job in many ways. That service is immensely affected by whether the chair is developing or achieving as a scholar.

Professional activities or retooling as a scholar might be less important for an individual who aspires to a higher administrative position after serving as chair. If a chair's career direction is unknown, it is best to keep both options open: to remain active professionally in scholarly activities and to learn as much as possible about academic leadership.

Extensive administrative time demands make it difficult to maintain an edge as a scholar or teacher. Whether the desired career path is administration, teaching, or research, consider the advice of one chair to "save time for yourself and maintain some degree of equilibrium in your own work." This calls for an agenda. Careful attention to scheduling classes and meetings can create blocks of time for concentrated scholarly activities and for teaching. Scheduling time for scholarly work was emphasized by one chair with eight years of experience in the hard sciences at a doctoral-granting school:

Chairs must learn to organize their time. One can always find things to do—shuffle papers, make another report. It's very important that a chair have a project always hanging overhead that will keep him in touch with his profession. It could be a research project or something administrative, but something where continuous ideas are needed.

When will you say you have finished your work as a chair? A useful exercise for chairs as they begin their tenure is to project ahead for a period, possibly five years, and imagine a going away party as a way to determine what you will be remembered for. Hopefully it will be more than "Thank goodness the SOB is gone!" In situations we have observed through training workshops, chairs comment on several aspects of their work that make them proud: fairness, a positive and caring culture, excellent programs, teaching, research and students, and improvement in departmental standing (for a more detailed discussion of the satisfaction of the job, see Gmelch & Burns, 1993).

If chairs take this exercise to heart, the stated goals and outcomes will become the focus of everyday and long-term actions and decisions. For example, if a chair wants to be known for facilitating a positive, caring culture, then attention to collegiality and civility, conflict management and empathetic response should receive everyday attention. In short, if one pays attention every day to these aspects, the outcomes are much more likely to be achieved. Otherwise it is too easy for the chair to be diverted from the reasons for taking the position in the first place.

One way of thinking about the question of when it is time to leave is to ask yourself if you have achieved the outcomes and no longer have others to motivate you. In short, has the challenge gone? Another consideration is that the stage of the department's development might suggest a different kind of leader would further its development. For example, a department might need a period of consolidation following major changes, or it might require a focus on entrepreneurial activity following a period of quality improvement. We take up considerations of resource development and quality improvement in later chapters.

Conclusion

As you embark on your personal professional development journey, you might wish to consider the following questions:

- What will be your legacy in the department?
- How will you balance your life? What will balance mean?
- When will you be finished with your chairing?
- What will happen to the leadership of the department in five years? What will you do to prepare it for that time?
- How will you prepare the next department chair?

Without a definite agenda, administrative tasks can consume much time. Creating equilibrium between one's career discipline and the duties of chairing a department is difficult because the demands of leadership always exceed the time available. Thus, exemplary chairs advised their colleagues to plan for the future by choosing a career path, maintaining a focus on intellectual work or retooling, and scheduling time for professional, discipline-based activities.

Endnotes

1. The Multifactor Leadership Questionnaire was developed by Bass and Avolio, and is based on their research on "full range leadership," which encompasses transformational, transactional, and laissez-faire styles. The DiSC Personal Profile System employs a four-factor cognitive map for understanding behavioral styles. The Myers-Briggs Type Indicator is a widely adopted personality profile

system based on 16 profiles. The StrengthsFinder, based on Gallup's StrengthsQuest model, employs 180 paired comparisons and produces a signature theme report that identifies a person's top five leadership characteristics.

2. Appreciative inquiry is a process that was developed by David Cooperrider and his associates, which is strengths-based and builds on multi-stakeholder cooperation.

3. Gmelch, W. H. (2006, January). Stress management strategies for academic leaders. *Effective Practices for Academic Leaders, 1*(1), 2. This newsletter is an excellent resource for chairs. It covers topics of current interest and provides useful advice. See Suggested Resources for further information.

Suggested Resources

Books and Periodicals

Chu, D. (2006). *The department chair primer: Leading and managing academic departments.* Bolton, MA: Anker.

    The author provides an overview of the various issues and perspectives on chairing. Each chapter is geared to job functions and responsibilities with specific suggestions for success. Each chapter ends with questions to consider. This book is definitely a starting point for chairs.

Diamond, R. M. (Ed.). (2002). *Field guide to academic leadership.* San Francisco, CA: Jossey-Bass.

    This book is a comprehensive guide that addresses higher education roles and responsibilities as well as important issues. There are chapters that speak to the roles of presidents, vice chancellors, deans, chairs, and faculty. An array of written and electronic resources is also included.

Eble, K. E. (1986). Chairpersons and faculty development. *The Department Advisor, 1*(4), 1–5.

    Eble was one of two contributors to this issue of *The Department Advisor.* Eble reports and reflects on his examination of chairs and their interests in faculty development at 41 colleges in Minnesota, North Dakota, and South Dakota. Traditional faculty development practices are discussed. Eble recommends chair involvement in faculty development, an involvement extending beyond traditional sabbaticals, travel funds, and grant writing support. After discussing the reasons people become chairs and the skills necessary for the position, he suggests ways that chairs should work with faculty members (e.g., let faculty members know that their work is important, let them know that they are contributing to the department and the institution).

Gmelch, W. H., & Schuh, J. H. (Eds.). (2004). *New directions for higher education: No. 126. The life cycle of a department chair.* San Francisco, CA: Jossey-Bass.

This volume identifies, examines, and analyzes selected issues related to the career development of the department chair with a special focus on how colleges and universities can assist faculty in preparing themselves for this difficult role and how chairs can be supported during their terms of service by their department and institution. The chapter authors examine how chairs can continue to develop their skills while serving in this leadership role and how they can prepare themselves for academic life after they conclude their administrative duties as chair.

Hecht, I. W. D. (2006, March). Becoming a department chair. *Effective Practices for Academic Leaders, 1*(3), 1–16.

Hecht has organized the American Council on Education's chair workshops for many years. She provides perspectives and sage advice on taking the chair position. She also provides examples of the candidates' motivation, an in-depth picture of what the position is about, and some resources for gaining greater understanding.

Hecht, I. W. D., Higgerson, M. L., Gmelch, W. H., & Tucker, A. (1999). *The department chair as academic leader.* Phoenix, AZ: American Council on Education/Oryx Press.

The authors have provided an update to Allan Tucker's classic book based primarily on the American Council on Education's workshops with chairs, their own extensive experience, and current literature. The four areas highlighted are roles and responsibilities, the department and its people, the department and its operations, and the department and the university. The book provides a historical review of important reference materials and the institutional context for chairs.

Henry, R. J. (Ed.). (2006). *New directions for higher education: No. 134. Transitions between faculty and administrative careers.* San Francisco, CA: Jossey-Bass.

This comprehensive guide provides an overview of various issues in the transition between faculty and administrative careers. This book should be required reading for any faculty member who is considering the transition from a faculty to an administrative career.

Kimble, G. A. (1979). *A departmental chair's survival manual*. New York, NY: Wiley.

Gregory Kimble wrote this book for chairs of psychology departments. It resulted from workshops conducted by the Council of Graduate Departments of Psychology. However, the content is pertinent to all disciplines. Readers will be amused, elated, or saddened by Kimble's observations. The introductory "Letter to a New Chairman" is particularly enlightening. It contains 14 lessons starting with: "As head of a department, you must be prepared to budget between one-fourth and one-half of your time for the totally unexpected" (p. 4).

Tucker, A. (1992). *Chairing the academic department: Leadership among peers* (3rd ed.). Phoenix, AZ: American Council on Education/Oryx Press.

Tucker offers an extensive discussion of the role of chairing an academic department. First published in 1981, *Chairing the Academic Department* benefited from Tucker's extensive experience conducting workshops (sponsored by the American Council on Education) for department chairs. The book covers the spectrum of departmental responsibilities and has become a classic in the field. We recommend special attention to the chapters on faculty development, evaluation, performance counseling, and grievances.

Wergin, J. F. (2003). *Departments that work: Building and sustaining cultures of excellence in academic programs*. Bolton, MA: Anker.

This book provides a helpful perspective on thinking about what the department is about (purposes, processes, and methods of evaluation). For the beginning or experienced chair, it raises fundamental questions for consideration and provides examples of effective departments.

Newsletters

Academic Leader

Academic Leader is a monthly publication that provides practical tips about chairing departments and brief discussions of research studies.

The Department Advisor

This newsletter is published four times per year by Higher Education Executive Publications, Inc. in affiliation with the American Council on Education, Center for Leadership Development. It includes original articles "providing concrete analyses and practical advice to help department chairs do their jobs."

The Department Chair: A Resource for Academic Administrators

This is a quarterly newsletter that highlights higher education issues with articles contributed by practicing administrators and higher education specialists. Articles address the litany of issues, functions, and responsibilities of chairs. Individual subscriptions or a site license are available from Jossey-Bass at www.josseybass.com.

Effective Practices for Academic Leaders: A Stylus Briefing

Effective Practices is a monthly publication "that assists leaders to better manage their work agendas and make key decisions by offering critical advice and information in a concise format for ready application in administrative life." It offers a range of topics in a 16-page format, including becoming a department chair, stress management, fostering scholarly research, the challenges and opportunities of technology, faculty development programs, and change management.

National Workshops

Kansas State University's Division of Continuing Education hosts the annual Academic Chairperson Conference (www.dce.k-state.edu/conf/academicchairpersons/). Also, the American Council on Education's Department Leadership Programs provides periodic workshops for department chairs (www.acenet.edu/AM/Template.cfm?Section=chairs_workshop). In addition, The Chair Academy sponsors an annual conference and academy particularly focused on skills needed by chairs, deans, and other organizational leaders in community colleges and four-year institutions (www.mc.maricopa.edu/community/chair/).

3

Reflect on Your Role as an Academic Leader

And another thing. I'm tired of everyone calling you Alexander the Pretty Good.

—A Gary Larson cartoon caption

Managing in an academic institution is a lot like managing a cemetery. You have plenty of people beneath you, but no one ever listens.

—Anonymous

As department chair your responsibilities extend beyond simply handling administrative tasks on behalf of the faculty. You are also an academic leader whose responsibilities include fostering a positive and productive work environment and attaining agreed-upon personal and departmental goals. As you progress in your role, you need to consider the strategies you can use to assist the entire department to grow and develop so that both faculty members' careers and departmental goals are enhanced.

Part of your challenge as a chairperson is to establish that sometimes delicate balance between the individual interests of faculty and the collective needs of the department. As highly skilled professionals, faculty expect and often demand high levels of autonomy. As members of professional associations, research teams, and communities of practice, faculty members often have what we might term *distributed loyalties*. In fact, their primary loyalty might not be to the department or even to the institution.

You might have to work patiently and deliberately as you seek out those valuable intersections between faculty members' professional aspirations and the department's needs. You have to build consensus concerning the major directions of the department and identify the resources required to support the various faculty initiatives that contribute to those directions. You also have to attend to the often overlooked dimension of the process, and that is the need to chart individual and departmental progress toward attaining their shared goals. Finally, you need to recognize the achievements and ensure that others are aware of the accomplishments.

This chapter provides you with several strategies you might consider as you assume your role as an academic leader in your department. As you read this chapter, you might wish to reflect on the following five questions:

- How do chairs work with faculty to develop a collective vision or focus for the department?
- How do chairs develop faculty ownership of the vision?
- How do chairs initiate change, given that change is an ongoing process?
- How do chairs acquire and use resources to help implement the vision and departmental goals?
- How do chairs monitor the progress of the department and individual faculty members in achieving the goals?

Establish a Collective Departmental Vision or Focus

Two national authorities on leadership, Bennis and Nanus (1985), describe vision as a "mental image of a possible and desirable future state of the organization. . . . [It] may be as vague as a dream or as precise as a goal or mission statement" (p. 89). Chairs we interviewed described vision as "an active focus on the future rather than the past"; "keeping in mind one axiom—what will be the best for the department, the students, and the curriculum over the long haul"; and "setting sights on long-term goals, recognizing that a chair can get pushed in so many different directions."

In gaining a collective commitment, Kouzes and Posner (2003) provide a useful insight:

> You can't impose a vision on others. It has to be something that has meaning to them, not just to you. Leaders must foster conditions under which people will do things because they want to, not because they have to. One of the most important practices of leadership is giving life and work a sense of meaning and purpose by offering an exciting vision. Leaders create environments where departmental (institutional) visions and personal values interact. (p. 34)

As important as it is to have inspiring long-term goals, it is also very beneficial to focus on the development of specific, practical, and achievable actions that contribute to goal attainment. As you work through the planning process, you might remind yourself of the admonition that "a vision without action is merely a dream."

One way to ensure that your department's vision does not fade over time is to link it to the mission of the institution and to its long-term goals. In this context you should ask yourself several related questions. What is the current focus of the college or university? Historically, what have been the major thrusts of the college or university? What has the college or university identified for future directions? What types of programs will be supported internally and externally? Answering these questions requires a clear vision of the mission of the unit and the entire institution. Without this, chairs said, "false expectations and unrealistic goals can be established for the faculty and for the department, which can result in conflict and lack of support from upper administration." Instead, chairs must "help [the faculty] understand and appreciate the mission of the institution."

Although faculty members need freedom to pursue individual career interests, those individual pursuits must be linked and related in a meaningful way to the broader institutional mission. Like the conductor of a symphony, chairs orchestrate the resolution of needs and the setting of priorities for the enhancement of individual and institutional goals. This dynamic was described by the chair of an education department at a comprehensive college:

> Faculty must have freedom to determine where their efforts will be expended. There are many things a faculty member can do to satisfy the individual as well as bene-fit the institution. The job of the administrator is to help determine ways faculty can help themselves and simul-taneously help the institution. The chair is in a key posi-tion to make this happen.

Faculty members experience satisfaction when their efforts are appreciated at the institutional level and when senior administra-tors view the faculty member's contributions as significant to the institution rather than as simply self-serving.

Develop Faculty Ownership of the Vision

A vision cannot be determined unilaterally by the chair because the academy is built on a foundation of participation and involvement of faculty in matters related to governance, staffing, students, bud-geting, and academic programs. Bennis and Nanus (1985) empha-size the importance of a collegial process in the important task of developing a departmental vision:

> A vision cannot be established in an organization by edict or by the exercise of power or coercion. It is more an act of persuasion, of creating an enthusiastic and ded-icated commitment to a vision because it is right for the times, right for the organization, and right for the peo-ple who are working in it. (p. 107)

Tierney (2002) also believes that responsive institutions need the focus that good mission and vision statements provide:

> Mission and vision statements are important first steps on the road to improved, more responsive organizations for the 21st century. Creating and sustaining change involves an overarching framework for principles and practices. A mission statement is the blueprint that will energize faculty, staff and external constituents and enable us to get started and remain on track. Such a statement helps establish priorities for programs, budgeting, reward structures and a host of institutional activities. (p. 50)

Struggle a bit with your own thoughts and reactions to the following questions before reading the strategies of exemplary chairs:

- What changes are necessary within the department?
- What mechanisms and structures exist for generating ideas?
- How can I get faculty interested in considering and owning ideas?

Chairs informed us about several strategies that worked well for them. A biomedical engineering chair in a relatively small department visited with faculty before meetings and allowed everyone to state his or her views on issues. "I drop into offices, chatting huddle fashion," he said. "This way faculty come to meetings primed for the issue." The chair's visits with faculty in this department build consensus among the faculty members, contributing to ownership. And faculty in the department also supported this view:

> We have a good consensus on issues, but he still allows the department to outvote him. Before we meet, issues are brought up. We try not to let decisions be made on a close vote. [The chair] goes around and talks before the meeting. We're generally aware of opportunities, and he

makes assignments based on interests and strengths. When we have a faculty meeting he doesn't say, "I am the head and this is what we will do." He sets the spirit and runs these meetings through consensus. Clockwise around the table, everyone comments, and then we reach a consensus. If consensus doesn't emerge, the decision is put off until more time can be spent considering it.

There are several strategies that can assist in building consensus. Simple brainstorming augmented by techniques such as forced choice exercises or nominal group process can be very effective in creating focus and moving beyond impasse. Building ownership through a consensus model at meetings was only one approach recommended and might be more viable in small to moderate sized departments.

Another strategy came from an education chair at a liberal arts institution who emphasized the importance of a nondirective approach:

Anyone who comes with an agenda, a leadership vision of what faculty ought to be, will have a hard time. There will be resistance to that management style. You need to listen to faculty; they are professionals. They know their own areas best. The chair, in my opinion, needs to represent and be responsive to faculty rather than be directive.

Another person we interviewed emphasized the role of the chair as a catalyst:

You can't do it by yourself. You need faculty support for developing a vision. Some faculty committee or group of committees must be given responsibility to assist with development. There's no way I could run all the programs in this department. The ownership of ideas has to be in the hands of faculty.

The ownership of ideas through faculty initiation was reinforced by a chair at a research institution who said, "Don't do anything your faculty did not initiate. Remember the bubble-up theory— nothing should be done that doesn't come from the faculty." Faculty feel ownership when they see some benefits for themselves. A chair in a large university department commented:

> The department has to be a unit with everyone working together, moving forward together, benefiting together, although in different ways depending on individual needs and interests. Some faculty might not see benefits immediately or how the program contributes to their development at a given point in time, but eventually they must be able to see the implications.

One person emphasized the importance of identity and social contacts in building ownership in a large department of 90 faculty at a research institution:

> We've tried to do things to keep a sense of cohesive community working together in a department of this size. We've posted everybody's picture along with their area of responsibility in a prominent place in the department. This might sound trivial, but people have been pleased. In addition, we started having informal social hours every few weeks. People just drop in and talk to one another. These practices actually seem to enhance people's sense of belonging to a group rather than just coming in and doing their thing and then going home.

A chair of a theater department at a major university shares his vision on a regular basis with his faculty:

> The chair of a department of theater is also the artistic director of the theater program. Thus, I believe in not only having a vision for the program but also sharing that vision. One way I share this vision is to write to my

faculty on a regular basis my thoughts about our departmental vision. I have—at least every semester—a meeting in which we talk simply about vision. As we have become increasingly trusting and ready to engage in discussion, I've discovered that my desire to share has been quite infectious.

These comments make it clear that chairs who are successful in developing faculty ownership are likely to elicit support and commitment.

Initiate Changes Carefully

Be thoughtful and cautious about making immediate changes. Allow sufficient time to let ideas mature and develop naturally. Most departmental procedures have a long history, but changes are sometimes required if the vision or direction of the department needs to be altered. Chairs advised that there are "no quick fixes." This sage advice contradicts the popular "100-day theory" in management circles—that is, to make changes during the "honeymoon" period.

The following quotes provide specific suggestions about change, including getting acquainted, listening, moving slowly, and making one change at a time:

> Hang loose. Spend time observing and getting acquainted. Do not do too much in the first year. Set plans. Don't apply formulas until you know what you're dealing with. Praise people; listen to them. Get acquainted with the faculty and the department before you decide what needs to be done. (A social sciences chair with 10 years of experience)

> Don't change too much too soon. If you don't have an administrative background, it takes at least a year to become familiar with your responsibilities. Visit with

other chairs to see how they handle various situations. Try to read as much as possible about management. (An accounting chair with 16 years of experience)

You can't change the world overnight. It takes six months just to figure out what is important to the faculty and the department. (A psychology chair with 8 years of experience)

Try not to build Rome in a day. The task of changing the department is too big to be accomplished in a short period of time. Look at departmental change as a long-term commitment. Take progress as it comes, capitalizing on the opportunities that emerge. (A chair in medicine with 8 years of experience)

The advice from the exemplary chairs who we interviewed was consistent:

- Let ideas and initiatives evolve progressively, but do not force or impose change.
- Spend time the first year observing and getting acquainted.
- Visit with other chairs to see how they handle situations.
- Look at any new "vision" as a long-term commitment.

Being careful and deliberate, however, does not mean abnegating responsibility for bringing about change. Chairs were firm in their counsel to take action immediately when it is warranted by a situation. It is also important to understand what has to be changed and help others to see the importance and, often, the urgency. The following example provided by an interviewee captures the essence of the question that chairs should ask themselves:

When I took over the department as chair, if someone had asked me, "Would you advise your daughter to start an undergraduate program in the department? Would you be happy with the education she would receive? Would you be happy with the environment? Would you be happy with the culture? Would you be comfortable in having the current faculty spend four years educating your daughter?" The answer to these [hypothetical] questions was "no." Yet I was expected to go out and recruit other people's sons and daughters and try and convince them to come and enroll in one of our programs. I said I am not going to recruit students into programs that I don't think are up to standard. It was only after we had hired some new faculty, reinvigorated existing faculty, revised the curriculum, refined the assessment process and procedures, and improved the physical facilities that I could say "yes." Because I knew they would get a quality education, they would be instructed by faculty with the right attitude, who were enthusiastic about their discipline and would have up-to-date classrooms and laboratories in terms of technology and equipment.

When we interviewed chairs in the late 1980s, they indicated that they were determined to have a solid understanding of the department and to move slowly and deliberately in making changes. Yet some experts suggest that the major issue facing higher education today is "effectively initiating, implementing and managing intentional, meaningful, planned change. In other words, the urgent need is for change creation" (Lick, 2002, p. 31). This need to create change was repeatedly identified as a high priority in the interviews conducted for this second edition.

Although we still suggest observing and listening to department members, chairs today find that they do not have the luxury of extended time in understanding and acting on issues that are critical to the department's well-being.[1] This change in perspective suggests that department chairs must be effective in sizing up issues quickly, framing them for the faculty, and mobilizing support for the action needed. Chairs must use their various spheres of influence—traditional and personal—to move toward a preferred vision of the future. The chair of a social science department at a land-grant university addressed the issue of the speed and nature of change in this way:

> The principal challenge is to get faculty to recognize that we live in changing times and that we as a department need to respond to circumstances. We need to be adaptable, we need to be flexible, and we need to have multiple constituencies.

Allocate Resources of Time, Information, and Assignments to Implement the Vision and Departmental Goals

Whether implementing changes or continuing along a steady course, academic leaders can exercise the power and influence of their positions to pursue a vision. While this power depends on many factors—foremost among them the degree of administrative latitude over the budget—most chairs exercise at least modest control over departmental resources such as funds, information, and faculty assignments. As one chair commented, "The most basic thing that any faculty member needs is the resources to do her work. That's my biggest responsibility."

The area of allocation of resources has changed significantly from the first edition of this book to the second. In fact so much has changed that a new chapter has been created, Chapter 11.

If a department has control over its budget, chairs can allocate funds to provide aid to faculty in the form of resources for secretarial assistance, costs for computers/technology, funds for travel, and resources for equipment purchases. Though exemplary chairs in our study talked about these traditional uses of funds, they also spoke about incentives, rewards, and equitable treatment of faculty. One chair did not mince words when speaking about incentives:

"Reward things that you want done." Others talked about allocating funds at the right place and time as incentives for faculty:

> Good management requires having resources in the right place at the right time. (A chair in an anthropology department with 22 faculty)

> Try to find resources that will enable people to do what they need to do. (A chair in a genetics department with 8 faculty)

> Give faculty resources so that they can maximize their effort. (A chair in a marketing department with 14 faculty)

Faculty can be rewarded through fair and equitable distribution of salary increases. This might involve negotiating faculty needs with senior administration. A chair in a languages and literature department at a doctoral-granting institution explained:

> You have to determine quickly the salary structure in the department. Determine how you can reward those faculty members who in previous administrations were not given the increments deserved—for whatever reasons. Then you have to convince the faculty and the dean it's a good idea to allow equity to prevail. Again, you will receive respect of the faculty—something that you need if you're going to be successful.

Chairs repeatedly emphasized the importance of being great "information givers," passing along information to faculty, which is another source of a chair's power and influence. The chair's office is a clearinghouse of materials of substantial interest to faculty: notices about meetings, announcements of available grants and contracts, and information about campus committees, events, and resources. The following advice gleaned from experienced chairs demonstrates the range of possibilities:

- When you have a feeling for what faculty prefer to do, you can start guiding materials toward them.
- Keep abreast of the periodicals and what is new. Pass this information along to the faculty.
- Try to put something in every faculty member's mailbox every day.
- Try to get as many sources of information as possible to your faculty.
- Help new faculty become aware of sources of support such as institutional resources and faculty aid programs.

Another resource for faculty is time to work on a favorite project, to take a "breather" from the routine of teaching or research, or to refocus efforts. Part of the difficulty in allocating this scarce resource is convincing senior administration of the need and the benefits. A chair in a doctoral-granting institution emphasized this point:

> I think you have to work very hard to convince the administration that faculty need released time in order to publish, research, and provide service. You also have to find ways to be flexible in providing time to the faculty member.

Numerous practices emerged from our interviews about managing time to the advantage of faculty. Sabbatical leaves and released time for additional graduate training, professional preparation, and research were the most often cited practices, but chairs also said:

- Assign first-year faculty members to teach in comfortable areas to lessen their load.
- Try to trade courses and research to get more teaching in a particular year and less teaching later.
- Try to avoid having too many faculty meetings.
- Try to get out of the way of faculty and let them do their jobs.

- Take administrative tasks from faculty so they can do their faculty jobs.
- Give individuals time off to attend workshops.

As this partial list suggests, you can augment traditional faculty development activities by allocating the time such development requires.

Monitor Progress Toward Achieving the Vision and Goals

Academic leaders also monitor individual and departmental progress toward long-term goals and a vision. To be effective, however, you must allocate resources to support key initiatives. Chairs should consider organizing procedures and data systems that indicate performance levels of faculty and staff. Responsibility for developing ownership and involvement by faculty in establishing and developing these systems often falls to the chairperson.

An effective database should be simple yet comprehensive and should cover the major activities in a department. Databases can become so complex and costly to maintain that they simply result in information overload. A chair of a biosciences department at a comprehensive institution offered several helpful suggestions:

> Get the departmental databases in order—for students, courses, published works, grants, and awards. Get on top of the problems with the curriculum. Sort out the new and emerging curriculum. Have a means to assess and determine those courses that need to be dropped.

Consider building a database of basic information about faculty performance. A chair in a special education department discussed collecting faculty data that would be accurate and representative of faculty work:

> Be adroit at picking information systems. Collect data
> on performance of the faculty, the effectiveness of the
> instruction provided by the department, the impact of
> resources provided, and the credit hour production. Try
> to be trusting while at the same time collecting data to
> document evidence of performance.

Faculty information has myriad uses, including pinpointing trends, tracing departmental history, and drawing comparisons both within the institution and with similar departments at other institutions. Instructional cost analysis reports—departmental and institutional—can assist chairs in making decisions about faculty assignments, the allocation of resources, and credit hours produced.

When the databases are developed, proper maintenance will ensure timely information for many purposes. Refreshing databases in the midst of a crisis is often too late. The systems are important not only in providing information and documenting performance but also in identifying potential problems. A biology chair at a research university spoke of this concern: "Know what is going on in the department so that you may head off potential problems before they emerge. You will be able to make better decisions." One of the most satisfying experiences for a chair is to have access to both summative and formative evidence documenting the progress of work toward specified objectives and goals.

Conclusion

This chapter has focused on the department chair's role as an academic leader. It has emphasized the importance of the role in providing focus and direction for individual and collective action; in promoting participation in the ongoing process of change; in using the resources and influence associated with the position to advance the change agenda; and establishing the metrics—quantitative and qualitative—to gauge the performance of individuals and the department as a whole against agreed-upon outcomes. Additional suggestions for leadership skills related to empowering faculty and processing feedback are included in Chapter 4.

As you contemplate your strategy for establishing clear departmental direction, you might wish to reflect on your answers to the following questions:

- Is the timing appropriate to engage the department in a serious goal-setting exercise?
- Do you have a process in mind and have you a clear sense of what you would like to see as the outcomes of the process?
- Do you have sufficient resources and support to undertake the process?
- Are there some short-term actions that could result in progress toward the goals that have been established?

Endnotes

1. Fortunately for change-conscious chairs, many faculty have also become aware of this collapsed time frame for action and have begun to understand that inaction can have serious consequences for the department. Discussion papers issued by the Pew Higher Education Roundtable and the American Association for Higher Education's New Pathways and Roles and Rewards initiatives, articles in *The Chronicle of Higher Education* and *Change*, and books such as Leslie and Fretwell's *Wise Moves in Hard Times: Creating and Managing Resilient Colleges and Universities* (1996) set the stage in the 1990s for major change that has continued in the present decade.

Suggested Resources

Heider, J. (1985). *The Tao of leadership: Leadership strategies for a new age*. New York, NY: Bantam.

The slow, natural enactment of change in a department is exemplified in this brief and entertaining book about leadership advice drawn from the writings of Lao Tzu, whose *Tao Te Ching* is a book of wise sayings, many of which will be familiar to you. Heider includes 81 lessons, such as "Selflessness," "Unbiased Leadership," "Take it Easy," "Gentle Interventions," and the "Unfolding Process."

Kouzes, J. M., & Posner, B. Z. (2003). *Jossey-Bass academic administrator's guide to exemplary leadership*. San Francisco, CA: Jossey-Bass.

Kouzes and Posner provide an insightful addition to the extensive array of management and leadership literature. Part Three, especially "Inspiring a Shared Vision," is recommended. The authors emphasize the steps involved in visualizing an ideal future and in sharing the vision with members of your organization. The book focuses on five essentials of leadership: model the way, inspire a shared vision, challenge the process, enable others to act, and encourage the heart.

Morris, J. (2007). The current leadership crisis and thoughts on solutions. In T. C. Mack (Ed.), *Hopes and visions for the 21st century* (pp. 250–263). Bethesda, MD: World Future Society.

Morris identifies five insights: the ability to see and influence systems, the confidence to make a difference, comfort with complexity and change, self-awareness and personal mastery, and passion and timing. In addition he lists four shoulder traits that bridge the gap between the insights: compassion, vision, purpose, and innovation.

Nanus, B. (1992). *Visionary leadership: Creating a compelling sense of direction for your organization*. San Francisco, CA: Jossey-Bass.

This book is helpful for chairs who are interested in the concept of vision and setting goals for an organization. Nanus provides a structure and process for developing and implementing visions that relate to departmental or unit concerns without ignoring the larger organizational context. Implementing a vision requires modeling behaviors and providing active support for the vision. He suggests establishing a vision or agenda that will focus the attention of everyone in an organization. For a detailed account of the process of visioning, consult Nanus's *The vision retreat: A participant's workbook* (1995).

4

Create a Positive Interpersonal Work Environment

*One doesn't have the option of choosing to ignore or
pull away from faculty. Choices are more limited.
The question is how to interact.*
　　　　　　　　　　—A chair of an education department
　　　　　　　　　　　　at a research university

*Find out what's going on out there and play to it.
Support it. Nurture it. Utilize techniques that are
appropriate to the personalities and the characteristics
of the faculty you're working with. There is no universal formula. You have to individualize.*
　　　　　　　　　　—A chair of a philosophy department
　　　　　　　　　　　　at a research institution

Always busy places, academic departments have experienced a
quickening of pace in the years since the first edition of this
Handbook appeared in 1990. The rapid proliferation of information
and the development of technologies that provide ever-increasing
access and ease of dissemination to the world's information resources
are but two of the forces shaping the current environment of academic departments. The steadily changing demographic profile of the
nation, increasing competition and consumer behavior, declining
levels of funding, and demands for greater accountability are some

of the other factors that, while present in the 1980s, have become much more pronounced in recent years.

Life in the academy is not what it was a generation ago. The sheer pace of life in departments today causes many faculty to focus on their own needs and interests, often at some expense to the development of community in departments. The need to focus on resources and results often works against communication and consensus building within the group. All of these emerging trends in the academic workplace create new challenges for department chairs whose job it is to recruit, retain, and support their faculty in this fundamentally changed environment.

This chapter provides chairs with strategies designed to create a positive work environment that contributes to faculty and departmental success and satisfaction. The chapter begins with a brief set of guiding principles to help frame the discussion of this topic, followed by a set of tools to assist in establishing a positive and productive working environment. These principles and the related tools should assist you in reflecting on your personal responses to such questions as:

- How do I establish an open atmosphere that will build trust with faculty and lead to a positive work environment?
- What steps are involved in listening to faculty needs, interests, and aspirations?
- How do chairs motivate faculty to excel and assist faculty in setting professional goals?
- What type of leadership empowers faculty? How do chairs provide positive feedback that enhances faculty self-esteem?
- How do chairs advocate for and represent faculty to colleagues and senior administrators?
- How do chairs act as role models or mentors for faculty?
- How do chairs encourage and support faculty?

Establish an Open Atmosphere to Build Trust

> It is important to create and maintain a collaborative, open, fair atmosphere, one in which there is a sense of caring about the development of the faculty as a primary function of the job. The chair has a lot to do with the atmosphere that is established. (A chair at a liberal arts college)

Though faculty members vary considerably in needs and abilities to contribute to a supportive environment, chairs can promote a positive, open departmental atmosphere. One chair called it "atmospheric guidance." This point was aptly stressed by a chair in a chemical engineering department at a doctoral-granting institution: "Set the proper framework and appropriate work environment so that faculty have a positive attitude toward their jobs."

What constitutes this framework? Excellent chairs talked about openness, trust, and honesty. Openness means creating a situation where faculty are free to express their views without threat of retaliation or reprisal. The chairs cited several ways to achieve or maintain openness, including respecting minority views, seeking everyone's input, keeping faculty informed about what is going on, avoiding the perception of competing with faculty, and being forthright in discussing institutional expectations with faculty. The chair of a department of civil engineering at a research university used the metaphor of a family to describe a workplace where faculty freely share their ideas: "Consider the environment of the department as a family. All are equally important to the whole system. Ask their help to be a part of the enterprise and help fine-tune it. Everyone's input should be respected." Besides respecting input, chairs expressed the importance of participation and involvement: "Everyone should feel that they know what is going on and that they have a voice in it."

It is difficult to be open on all matters. The chair of a department of social sciences in a liberal arts college described his frustrations: "The chair has a continuing responsibility to maintain openness with the faculty. However, it is extremely difficult because you constantly find yourself being pressured to make quick decisions on items that need faculty discussion."

Previous research has discovered several interesting concepts that are important in creating a positive work environment. Barrow and Davenport (2002) found in the private sector that the following were important conditions for fostering a positive environment:

- Recognition of work
- Involvement in change
- A job "that gets the best out of me"
- Role clarity
- Consultation
- Management that motivates

An open, trusting, and honest atmosphere promotes a positive work environment and a spirit of collegiality. Chairs can build this spirit through genuine attempts to share decision making, respect individual views, keep faculty informed about expectations and what is going on, and let them share in making decisions. All of these practices promote an open atmosphere in the department and help to build trusting relationships with faculty.

Dealing with conflict is a necessary and crucial aspect of creating a positive culture. People have differences, and these can either be seen as problematic or an invitation for growth and understanding. Cheldelin and Lucas (2004) identify four levels of conflict analysis and provide examples for chairs to gain perspective.[1]

Listen to Faculty Needs and Interests

Most of us can profit from improving our listening skills. As a chair, you might find that faculty are reluctant to talk freely with you because of experiences with past leaders who did not listen or who were unwilling to accept differences of opinion. Extra effort might be required to help faculty feel comfortable sharing their true thoughts. A basic principle of exemplary chairs is to "reach out to each faculty member, not just to the complainers or to those supporting your views." A political science chair at a doctoral-granting school said, "I would listen, listen, listen. My strongest piece of advice is to keep your door open and reach out to each faculty member—even the ones whom you think are doing well."

You might wish to consider the following list of active listening skills that most people respond to positively:

- *Put the individual who is talking to you at ease.* Start the conversation by discussing an area of common interest, have open body language, lean slightly forward as the person is speaking, maintain eye contact, and take notes as the person speaks.
- *Focus on central ideas.* Good information is available if you listen for it. Listen for major ideas and themes. Sort evidence from opinion, fact from principles, and ideas from examples. What is the individual really wanting to communicate?
- *Keep an open mind.* While listening, "Appreciate and tolerate different points of view" (an anthropology chair at a comprehensive college). Keep an open mind and ask questions rather than make statements to clarify your understanding. "Know when to be silent and when to provide input" (a health sciences chair at a doctoral-granting school). You might want to jot down points to rebut later, and phrase these points as questions.
- *Write down the ideas and later reflect on them.* One final recommendation from the chair of an anthropology department at a comprehensive college is to "Listen more. Write it down. Mull it over. Then reflect on what it means. The act of writing it down improves your ability to remember the speaker's major points."

Motivate Faculty and Collaboratively Set Goals

Creating an environment that is not only positive but that is also motivating to faculty can greatly enhance the ability of the department to reach its goals. Faculty who enjoy their work environment and who are motivated can accomplish almost anything.

There are many theories of human motivation, and whatever motivational theory you subscribe to, be it Maslow's hierarchy of motivational needs, Hertzberg's motivator/hygiene factors, or Vroom's expectancy theory, an understanding of motivational theory is helpful in creating a positive work environment. When faculty feel motivated there will be a palpable sense of excitement. The value of motivation to faculty productivity cannot be underestimated. Motivation is an individual issue and, therefore, requires a personal knowledge of each faculty member. Because motivation is unique to individuals and groups, a discussion with faculty individually and as a group will help you understand what they want their department to be like and what they expect from their chair. However, as the chair you need to recognize that you can only create the conditions for motivation to occur. Although there are no simple or foolproof prescriptions for how to create an "open" environment and increase the motivation of faculty, according to McCaffery (2004, pp. 164–165), there are several guiding principles to remember when thinking about motivating faculty:

- There is no magic formula: No simple lever, least of all money, maintains or increases motivation, specifically in professional organizations such as universities.
- Success, as ever, lies in the details: It minimizes the dissatisfiers and maximizes the motivators. The motivational climate of your department is literally the sum total of all the pluses and minuses of the various individual factors on both sides of the equation. As such, it is essential that you consider all of the factors influencing dissatisfaction and enthusiasm.

- Continuity and consistency: Establishing a positive motivational climate takes time, it does not happen overnight, and it requires constant attention. Almost everything you do has motivational consequences. You should, therefore, always attempt to anticipate the effects and, equally importantly, the side effects of your actions. Thus, the introduction of a new system aimed at cost saving, for example, will not secure the maximum positive effect if the process of complying with it is perceived as excessively bureaucratic and time consuming. Indeed, the lasting motivational effect might well be a negative one.

- Differences in timescale: Motivation and performance levels do not rise and fall together. Rather, performance always follows motivation. Thus, if you are attentive, you might be able to prevent a drop in motivation that adversely affects levels of performance. Equally, you need to be patient and avoid overreacting if initiatives you take do not instantly yield the desired effect.

- Always keep others in mind: The things that motivate or concern your colleagues might not be ones you value. Equally, what you believe is important might not be important to others. However, it is what they value that counts. You must be careful, therefore, not to simply dismiss their suggestions. If you do, you will be regarded as uncaring, and you might miss the opportunity to improve your motivational effectiveness.

Helping faculty set professional goals can be a rewarding experience for both you and the faculty member. By listening closely, chairs can gain an understanding of each faculty member's needs and concerns and can then help to connect those with departmental and institutional goals. However, it is important to avoid making assumptions about faculty needs. The chair of a political science department made the following recommendation:

> I sit down with each faculty member individually and have extended conversations with them about how they feel about the department, their role within the department, and their goals, both short- and long-range. Then I work out in my own mind and write down two or three things that I want to do for each member of the department to improve their morale, solve some problem, or remove some irritant they have identified as an obstacle.
>
> You don't want to make assumptions about what colleagues want for their professional growth and development. You want to find out from them what they perceive their needs to be. Only after you have a clear, concise sense of what their concerns are, should you set about trying to assist them.

It is important to set realistic goals. If the faculty member has not been very productive, you cannot expect immediate improvement. The chair of a language/literature department stated, "I help faculty develop clear, concise, realistic goals with a timeline for accomplishing them. You have to be realistic. You can't expect a person who hasn't done much for five years to suddenly bloom into something outstanding." Collaboratively setting goals with faculty involves visiting with them to diagnose their needs, linking individual goals to departmental goals and the institutional mission, checking to make sure that individual plans are realistic, and then helping faculty members say "no" to peripheral involvements so they can realize their goals.

Develop Leadership Skills that Empower Faculty and Provide Effective Feedback

Leadership can have a considerable impact on the motivational climate of a work environment. As Kouzes and Posner (2003) point out, "the domain of leaders is the future" (p. xiii). The leader's style affects the environment in significant ways. As a chair, it might be helpful to ask: "What kind of leadership qualities are needed to empower faculty to move our current department toward a future we envision?" "What kinds of feedback and communication skills are needed to build the self-esteem of faculty?" "What feedback processes will foster faculty performance in achieving our goals?"

In *The Higher Education Manager's Handbook*, McCaffery (2004, p. 66) describes his concept of a visionary leader who is able to empower others to excel at what they do. According to McCaffery, the behaviors, personal characteristics, and culture-building activities common to all effective transformational[2] leaders include the following features, which were corroborated by the chairs we interviewed.

Behaviors

- *Focus: Providing a clear focus on key issues and concerns* (i.e., doing the right things). As one chair at a state university commented, "We're primarily a teaching institution, so I think one of the things that helps teamwork is to have a focused kind of problem to solve. And so, where I see the teamwork working best is those places where people feel that they have that kind of common issue around which they can focus and sort of coalesce."

- *Communication: Getting everyone to understand this focus through effective organizational communication practices.* This communication can happen in a variety of ways, depending on the needs of the department. Some departments have a coffee hour or informal luncheons; others prefer a set time for meeting. As a chair at a state university remarked, "We meet each Wednesday morning as faculty and in some instances don't necessarily have a whole lot of things on the agenda, and so there's a lot of exchange that goes on for that hour or so."

Another chair from a state university prefers a more formal event: "We have an annual retreat. Before the academic year begins we can reflect on where we've been and then what some of our goals will be for the future year. And about midyear—sometimes we'll wait toward the end of the academic year—we might get together for a common luncheon or something like that where we don't have an agenda. It's just an opportunity to socially get together. And I think that actually helps to bind faculty somewhat."

- *Consistency: Acting predictably, over time, as a means of developing trust*. The chair of a geological environmental energy department at a public research university offered this advice: "Make sure your message is consistent because some people hang on every word. So you have this tremendous power, I guess that's not the right word. The influence that you have is really amazing, so you have to be careful how you express things."

- *Respect: Demonstrating care and respect for department members through thoughtful actions*. A chair of an educational philosophy and planning department at a state university made the case for establishing credibility on a firm base of trust: "The effectiveness of your work rests on how much currency you have with your colleagues in the department. Not how good an administrator you are, not how well connected you are with administrators. It is how much trust and relationship you have with your colleagues. If your colleagues lose faith in you, regardless of how effective you are, chances are you may have a very diminished role."

- *Empowerment: Creating empowering opportunities that involve the department's members in making the right things their own priorities*. A chair at a state university empowers faculty through an active and inclusive process:

"We go through a process of goal setting that involves the entire department once every two or three years. We revisit our goals and look to see where it is we want to make inroads, make improvements; and for the most part, the department works extremely well together to make that happen. They have a focused set of desires to be a very, very good instructional department."

Personal Characteristics

Cultivating certain personal characteristics can be very beneficial to you as a leader. Three particular attributes are most helpful:

- *Exhibiting self-confidence: A conviction of one's ability to make a positive difference.* A chair at a community college put it this way: "Maintain your own self-confidence and the self-esteem of others, maintain a relationship with them, take initiatives and make things better and lead by example."
- *Demonstrating a comfort level with empowerment: A belief in the ability of others to make a positive difference.* At a state research university a chair commented, "I go to them with a problem that I want their help to solve. I try to phrase things in that way. I try to say, here's the issue, how do *we* go about doing this? And if people give this sort of 'I' 'me' answer, I say, that's fine for you but that doesn't solve the problem for the department as a whole."

  Another chair at a state university said, "We may disagree about how we do that and then they argue with one another about how we do that, but the argumentativeness I liken to the French, [who] have a debate or discussion, and it may be spirited, but it is founded in thought rather than in emotion and opinion. So I think that the faculty are resourceful and, by and large,

I think they are committed to working extraordinarily hard for the highest possible quality."

- *Clarifying long-term directions: A commitment to the establishment of desirable goals and a roadmap to reach the destination.* A music department chair said, "My job as a leader is to inspire and excite people with the vision of where we could be and what we could be together. And that just takes energy everyday to be there."

Culture Building

Attention to the building of departmental culture is a very important component of leadership. It includes creating assumptions, values, and beliefs that support four key organizational functions: managing change, achieving goals, coordinating teamwork, and maintaining a vibrant organizational culture. A chair at a state research university said:

> We have a faculty colloquium where faculty give scholarly papers and we have wine and cheese, so that kind of social thing is another strategy for promoting collegiality. We set up clear procedures as a way to foster community so that everybody has a sense of how things are going to proceed and some people in the community don't have information that other people are not privy to.

Feedback Techniques

One of the most important and challenging tasks of a leader is to provide clear and constructive feedback to followers. Department chairs must provide regular feedback to faculty members regardless of whether performance is positive or needs improvement. Communicating honest feedback requires precision and tact in addition to well-honed interpersonal skills. A political science chair at a doctoral-granting institution said:

There is a tendency to give up on certain people. If you have somebody in his late 50s or 60s who hasn't done anything professionally and seems to be teaching from those old yellowed pages, there is a tendency to ignore that person and work around him. You really shouldn't neglect him.

Acknowledging that not all people can be helped, exemplary chairs we interviewed nevertheless stressed becoming involved with faculty and even confronting them when necessary. The faculty member might not realize there is a problem, as a chair in the hard sciences pointed out: "I visited with her about the student's complaints. At first she seemed shocked that there was a problem." A chair at another institution advised, "Start easy. The person needs a friend. Work on it together."

A noted authority on interpersonal skills, Lawrence Brammer (1979, pp. 86–88) discusses seven techniques that are useful in confronting individuals with evident performance problems:

- Give observations in the form of feedback when individuals are ready.
- Describe the behavior before giving your reaction to it.
- Give feedback about the behavior rather than judgments about the person.
- Give feedback about things that the person has the capacity to change.
- Give feedback in small amounts so that the individual can experience the full impact of your reaction.
- Give prompt feedback to current and specific behavior, not unfinished emotional business from the past.
- Later, ask the individual for reactions to your feedback. Did it enhance the relationship or diminish it?

Using feedback steps such as Brammer's, recognizing that faculty might not be aware of a problem, and confronting faculty when the situation merits it allow chairs to challenge individuals without diminishing their dignity and self-esteem.

Represent Faculty to Colleagues and Senior Administrators

Building positive relationships can be enhanced by chairs advocating on behalf of an individual faculty member with senior colleagues or administrators on campus. A psychology chair at a doctoral-granting school discussed this role:

> I have to say the only crucial thing is to be on the faculty's side. You have to be their advocate. You also must be your staff person's advocate. Chairs or faculty can't offend secretaries and still hope to get things done.

A chair of a psychology department at a doctoral-granting institution reinforced the concept of protection:

> I think it is very important that the department head establish the mental set within the department that the head is the departmental advocate. If the faculty don't perceive you as their advocate you have a very tough row to hoe.

The chair is typically a buffer between faculty and upper-level administration. A genetics chair at a research university talked about his role:

> The most important thing I can do is be a buffer between the faculty and the administration. I also try to keep the administrative responsibilities of faculty to an absolute minimum so the faculty can focus their time on teaching and research.

What does *buffering* mean? For one individual it means "taking the heat" from upper-level administration. A liberal arts college chair discussed just how challenging but important this role can be:

> The chair has to be willing to incur the wrath of higher administration. The chair's position is to argue as effectively as possible for the concerns of the faculty and the department. The chair needs to be the faculty voice to the administration.

The chair might indeed be the only voice that faculty have with administration; it is understandable, then, that faculty feel strongly about the chair's advocacy role. Walking the tightrope between being an advocate for faculty and supportive of the administration offers the department chair a unique challenge.

Serve as a Role Model and Mentor

One strategy used by chairs to gain the confidence of senior administrators as well as department faculty is to model high levels of performance and to mentor faculty toward attaining high levels of performance in their own right. Chairpersons who stressed the concept of role modeling described setting a good example for faculty:

> It's extremely important that the chair serve as a role model. Don't expect of others what you won't do yourself. For example, if there is a big concern about professional growth and development within a department, you shouldn't be the chairperson if you can't set the pace in that area. (A political science chair at a doctoral-granting school)

> Try to set a good example for the faculty in teaching, research, and faculty development in general. Get good marks in those areas yourself and its impact carries over

to your department, the institution, and off campus. (A sociology/anthropology chair at a comprehensive college)

The first thing I would do is model the behavior that I expect from others. If you want them to be productive and to participate in activities, you have to model that yourself. But you have to try to maintain some stability, working at a balance. (A special education chair at a research university)

Chairs need to keep standards for themselves that they hold for faculty, respect individual differences in faculty members, and encourage senior members in the department to serve as role models and mentors for junior faculty.

Encourage and Support Faculty

To help faculty reach high levels of performance, cultivate their individual strengths and encourage them in the areas in which they excel. A psychology chair at a liberal arts school combined assessing faculty strengths with encouragement:

Number one, you should concentrate on assessing your faculty's strengths and weaknesses. Two, encourage, encourage, encourage. Play on those strengths and almost ignore or minimize the weaknesses. Don't hone in on weaknesses. As an administrator, you can bring a positive perspective that others may not see.

There is no set pattern for support and encouragement. The chairperson of a health sciences department at a research university indicated that it is important to "follow your instincts about encouraging people to do their best." A chair of languages and literature at a doctoral-granting school used positive reinforcement and feedback: "You have to allow faculty to make a little progress at a time and keep encouraging them. Use positive reinforcement all the time, constant input, and feedback."

Effective chairs recognize the need to encourage all faculty. It is easy to give up, especially when there is little indication of an individual's progress or interest in trying to improve:

> Don't neglect the ones who seem to be doing fine; give them encouragement. Also, though it sounds preachy, don't give up on anybody. My own sense is that the "deadwood had gotten that way largely because they have been neglected." You should keep trying to know individuals in terms of their own aspirations and hopes for the department. There is often some way to rekindle some spark within them. (A chair of computer science)

This advice might sound simple or easy. It is not. It is a challenge to identify strengths or an area of interest where the faculty member is willing to invest time and energy. "It's not always easy to find where initiative lies in a faculty member," said a philosophy chairperson at a research university. "At the same time you encourage initiative, it must be done with restraint but some are overbearing."

Work hard to identify the strengths of the faculty, build on these strengths through encouragement, and work with all faculty—the producers and the nonproducers alike. When change does occur, be ready to provide encouragement and reinforcement.

Creating a positive interpersonal work environment involves establishing an open atmosphere where trust is built. It all begins with the chair who is the one who sets the tone for the culture of the department. When you feel positive about the work you do, your attitude will have a positive affect on others. As the chair of a physics department at a state university observed, "I think the big key is really to try to make it an open environment where faculty feel comfortable with each other and recognize good work."

Conclusion

A great working environment is developed by listening to faculty and understanding their needs. This helps you understand how to motivate them personally, and highly motivated faculty will have the inspiration needed to set professional goals that align with departmental and institutional goals. Developing your interpersonal communication skills for conversations about faculty performance and ways to frame those conversations to build faculty self-esteem will be a major benefit to your leadership. Advocating and representing faculty to the rest of the campus is vital. The behavior you model will speak much louder than your words in setting a tone for your department. Finding effective ways of encouraging and supporting faculty is also a key to creating a collegial environment.

As you contemplate the ways that you can motivate faculty and create a dynamic and productive work environment, consider these questions:

- What types of situations in your past work environments have motivated you to do your best?
- What types of situations in your past work environments have motivated others?
- What unique factors in your department are conducive to a positive work environment?
- What could be improved in the work environment and collegiality of your department?
- What steps can you take as chair to facilitate these improvements?

Endnotes

1. The four levels of conflict identified by Cheldelin and Lucas are:

   - Intrapersonal: impact of stress and negative thinking
   - Interpersonal: helping people who do not get along
   - Intragroup: academic administrator as team leader
   - Intergroup: conflict on a larger scale

2. The term *transformational leader* is often contrasted with *transactional leader*. It refers to a leader's ability to inspire followers to perform beyond expectations by creating challenging and productive goals and supporting individuals in their attainment of these goals. By contrast, transactional leaders rely on an exchange theory predicated on a system of rewards and punishments that are tied to specific performance measures.

Suggested Resources

Barrow, S., & Davenport, J. (2002). *"The employer brand," People in business.* Unpublished manuscript.

> Levels of "employer brand awareness" are rapidly increasing across Europe, North America, and Asia-Pacific as leading companies realize that skilled, motivated employees are as vital to their commercial success as profitable customers. Starting with a review of the pressures that have generated current interest in employer branding, this definitive work looks at the historical roots of brand management and the practical steps necessary to achieve employer brand management success, including the business case, research, positioning, implementation, management, and measurement. Case studies of big-name employer brand stories include Tesco, Wal-Mart, British Airways, and Prêt a Manger.

Brammer, L. M. (1979). *The helping relationship: Process and skills* (2nd ed.). Englewood Cliffs, NJ: Prentice-Hall.

> This book describes in nontechnical language the human helping process and provides training for anyone interested in becoming a helper. Filled with examples and step-by-step outlines for how to develop basic counseling skills, this book focuses on helping people learn to help themselves and each other. Providing a systematic approach to acquiring helping skills, this book cuts through psychological jargon and reaches across various professions and settings. Readers are asked to consider important personal issues of being a helper as they enter professional or paraprofessional roles as helpers.

Cheldelin, S. I., & Lucas, A. F. (2004). *Jossey-Bass academic administrator's guide to conflict resolution.* San Francisco, CA: Jossey-Bass.

> This book is a resourceful guide for higher education administrators interested in improving their conflict resolution skills. It offers tips for interpersonal conflict resolution as well as intrapersonal conflict resolution, which is often underestimated.

Kouzes, J. M., & Posner, B. Z. (2007). *The leadership challenge* (4th ed.). San Francisco, CA: Jossey-Bass.

This book provides a comprehensive explanation of the empirical and conceptual basis for the practices and behaviors that are the foundation of the Leadership Practices Inventory instrument. This research tool has been used to better understand the everyday actions and behaviors of exemplary leaders at all levels and across a variety of organizational settings. The book offers numerous suggestions for improving skills in these practices and behaviors.

McCaffery, P. (2004). *The higher education manager's handbook: Effective leadership and management in colleges and universities.* New York, NY: Routledge.

This volume seeks to inspire and guide academic and general managers alike who work in higher and further education. Based on the author's experiences and his research into higher education management in the UK and the US, the text examines the particular set of challenges facing anyone managing or moving into management in this complex environment. It addresses both the difficulties of managing in a sector traditionally hostile to overmanagement as well as the risks of outmoded approaches. Topics include the higher education context and challenge, knowing your institution, leading departments, managing for performance, and change in education.

Part II

Applying the Strategies

5

Help New Faculty Become Oriented

To ensure that the academic career remains a strong option for the capable, committed scholars we will need in the years ahead, we must understand and address its key problems: lack of a comprehensible tenure system, lack of community, and lack of an integrated life.

—Rice, Sorcinelli, and Austin, 2000

Having established in Part I the importance of the 15 strategies that chairs rely on in leading their departments, we now turn to the application of these generic strategies to specific issues that chairs confront on a daily basis. We begin with a host of issues related to recruitment, orientation, socialization, and support of new faculty. The greatest asset of any department is highly qualified faculty, and the greatest challenge for a department chair is finding effective means to recruit and retain the most highly qualified faculty. This key role is the responsibility of more than just the chair; the entire department needs to be a part of the development and retention of new faculty. This requires teamwork, a common vision for the future, and a commitment to continuous improvement within the department. Leadership on the part of the chair is what brings the department together in this undertaking.

As described by Gappa, Austin, and Trice (2007), faculty positions now are more differentiated beyond the classic tenure-leading positions with more fixed appointments and special appointments. They discuss the reasons for the changes and suggest that any appointment should create respect for and fairness to those in the positions.

In *Heeding New Voices,* Rice, Sorcinelli, and Austin (2000) suggest that "intellectual, social, and resource support from senior faculty, chairs, deans, and other campus administrators may be critical in attracting, developing, and retaining faculty" (p. 2). As the present faculty workforce ages, selects early retirement, or reaches retirement age in the next decade, an increasing number of new faculty will be joining academic departments. These new teachers and researchers will need to establish a sense of identity, ownership, and affinity with their departments. They might be recent graduates assuming their first teaching posts, experienced faculty moving from another institution, temporary appointees, or part-time staff promoted to full-time positions.

We must ask ourselves what are the needs and expectations of individuals during the first year or two of their careers in a new academic department. All faculty experience predictable phases of settling in, adjusting, and creating niches in academic units. You might reflect on your own early experiences as a new member of a department. This reflection can provide valuable insight into what to do and what to avoid when working with new staff. While considering your own experience, it is wise to consider as well the changes in culture and environment that might be relevant in your current academic department.

This chapter focuses on your role in assisting newly hired faculty in becoming acclimated to the culture of your department and integrated in a meaningful way into its mission and goal attainment. As with previous chapters, this one begins with a set of questions that draws on your own experience in new roles and institutions:

- What events or experiences assisted me in making my transition(s) to a new appointment?
- What supports did I find particularly valuable in establishing myself as a productive member of the new group?
- What was I particularly interested in knowing about in my new position?
- What would I consider doing differently now that the responsibility for socializing new members to the department rests with me?

Heeding New Voices (Rice et al., 2000) presents 10 principles of good practice in supporting new faculty based on the authors' interviews with new and early-career faculty.[1] These principles focus on ways to improve the review and tenure process; to encourage positive relations with colleagues and students; and to alleviate stress related to time and balance. The authors suggest that the 10 principles can act as a resource for developing your department's own plan. The principles they recommend are:

1. Communicate expectations for performance
2. Provide feedback on progress
3. Enhance collegial review processes
4. Create flexible time lines for tenure
5. Encourage mentoring and integration by senior faculty
6. Extend mentoring and feedback to graduate students who aspire to be faculty members
7. Recognize the department chair as a career sponsor
8. Support teaching, particularly at the undergraduate level
9. Support scholarly development
10. Foster a balance between professional and personal life

Communicate Expectations for Performance

A discussion about expectations can begin with the interview. Ask questions that allow you to understand the goals of the new faculty member and to determine if they align with your department goals. Include clear and precise communication in the letters of appointment and statement of expectations to help the new faculty member understand the expectations of your department. Review your tenure process, if you have one, with the candidate during the interview and early in his or her experience on campus. Be sure there are no surprises when the faculty member arrives on campus. However, there might be difficult questions regarding specific publication guidelines, particularly to obtain tenure, which cannot be answered at the time of the interview. Where there are ambiguities, explain them, and, if possible, set a date when those issues will be clarified. Met expectations are one of the best means of satisfying a faculty member.

When the new faculty member has arrived on campus, meet to determine that what is needed to succeed is in place and to clarify what you, the department, and the institution expect of the new faculty member. Also, recognize that new faculty might not always be aware of what he or she needs. This point was conveyed best by a physical sciences chairperson at a major research university:

> We ask [beginning faculty] for a very definite list of their needs. But you have to realize that we also know, perhaps better than they, what they're going to need. It's coaching them to what they really need. We have a very good idea of what it's going to take for a person's development.

During an early conversation with a new staff member, find out what that person perceives his or her needs to be. The following categorization of potential needs, drawn from the literature about new faculty, might be useful to organize your thoughts:

- Intellectual companionship
- Support and encouragement from colleagues

- Identification with the institution
- Knowledge about the formal and informal operations of the institution
- Knowledge about role expectations
- Released time to become oriented and adjusted to a new work situation

It might also be helpful to familiarize new faculty with the institution as a whole and to your department through formal and informal orientation processes. During this orientation, routine operating procedures and more subtle cultural expectations can be explained. New staff might view orientation as another hurdle before getting on with other tasks, but you should keep in mind that this is part of the preparation to prevent future problems. Remember that an orientation helps the individual identify with the institution and learn about its formal operation. It sends a message to faculty that they will be supported and encouraged. When done well, it builds faculty ownership for departmental goals and mission. How new faculty respond to an orientation program will be strongly affected by the attitudes of the faculty and chair. If they follow up and discuss concepts and information presented, the experience will be perceived to have been of value. If either the faculty or chair conveys the impression that orientation is a waste of time, it is unlikely that the new faculty member will value it. If the present orientation is ineffective, then you should urge that it become more useful or find effective alternatives.

If you are considering revamping your existing orientation program, you might wish to consult the following checklist for ideas about what to include:

- Responsibilities of the chair
- Responsibilities of the faculty
- Relationship of the department to the dean's office
- The faculty handbook
- Tenure and promotion criteria

- Academic standards
- Program and graduation requirements
- Grading procedures
- Services available for advising students
- The drop-and-add process
- Use of teaching assistants and research assistants
- Appeal and grievance procedures

In summarizing the orientation program at his institution, one chair commented:

> It is a full orientation session. It pays off. They don't remember everything, but it gives them a chance to ask questions and raise issues and to get a feel for the fact that they're going to be supported by their colleagues, their chair, and other personnel.

Departments with a small number of faculty can use other methods for orientation. For example, at small liberal arts colleges, deans often conduct formal programs while chairs support the deans by informally conveying the collegiate values, traditions, and history of the institution.

While the orientation of full-time faculty must, of necessity, be quite extensive, you might wish to consider implementing at least a basic orientation for your adjunct faculty. A chair at a community college told us:

> My administrative assistant and I have developed a CD that we use for our adjunct orientations so we don't have to have the same old routine every fall and spring semester for the adjuncts. They take the CD and look at it, view it, and I have developed a faculty handbook for all the sciences so that they have that. And [we also have] another little pocket size flip chart where they can have important telephone numbers and so on.

The orientation process is the first step in launching faculty on their new careers, and it deserves thoughtful planning and appropriate resources.

Provide Feedback on Progress

Feedback on progress toward tenure can occur at the annual review and also at regular conferences between you and the new faculty member throughout the year. The time set aside for this type of communication will have a high return rate. Be encouraging and supportive in this review process. Use these meetings as a listening time to find out about any unmet expectations the faculty member might have. Be honest, open, and encouraging about the future. Many institutions have found that bringing new faculty together provides opportunities to give support to one another and increases the learning for the group. Developing a cohort of new faculty that meets at a regular time can help to give valuable social and intellectual support to new faculty.

Look for tangible signs of adjustment and orientation and reinforce them during the pre-tenure years of a faculty member's service. Is the individual taking action to meet the needs identified as common to new faculty? Look for signs of growth, such as companionship, support, identification with the school, understanding of the institution and institutional expectations, and time-use skills. For example, signs of successful adjustment include developing new courses, recruiting students, publishing in journals, writing grant proposals, and setting up working laboratories.

Less tangible signs of success include positive attitudes and a sense of satisfaction with the department. As a chair of parks and recreation at a doctoral-granting university put it: "He obviously has to be very satisfied with what he is doing, and I think that satisfaction has been translated into his willingness to stay here and be part of this program." Similarly, a pharmacy chair at a major university observed: "I think that he has been more than willing to cooperate in the department in research and scholarship. He feels the sense of reward. I think he's moving along very well." Keep in mind that research with new faculty indicates that they desire both autonomy and collegiality. Disaffected or unhappy faculty often express disappointment that they have found autonomy but not collegiality and that they have had to find that outside the department in peer groups or communities of practice.

Enhance Collegial Review Processes

When new faculty see and hear an ongoing discussion in the department about the tenure process and the values that inform it, they will become not only better informed but also more motivated to be a part of the process. There are many ways of bringing attention to the review process. One chair at a community college described the system in this manner: "We have a process called an Individual Development Program here on campus through Staff Development. Each year it's updated and you set goals. You set short-range and long-range goals."

A clear set of guidelines for tenure review will enhance faculty understanding of the process. Bringing tenure-track faculty together for information sessions and inviting the pre-tenure faculty to attend will help them shape their approach to the tenure process. Some institutions hold a session with the tenure review committee and new faculty to begin communication about the tenure process; others invite new faculty to attend actual tenure review sessions to experience the tenure process firsthand. There are institutions that have promotion and tenure committees or other groups that provide regular feedback to faculty members on their progress, including recommendations for further development.

The chair of an education and childhood development department at a private university told us:

There are ongoing faculty development programs, actually multiple faculty development programs which are optional. Beginning faculty have a greater expectation to participate. Part of that helps the networking with other faculty members from other academic departments across campus and helps them in their pursuit of tenure to be better known by faculty outside of the department.

Create Flexible Time Lines for Tenure

Many institutions have become very creative in developing individualized time lines for tenure. They might allow for stopping the clock when a baby is born or counting previous work for credit toward early tenure. Research has shown that women and faculty of color might need special career guidance as they approach the tenure process. Additional load adjustments can be made just prior to tenure review. The more flexible the process, the more likely new faculty are to succeed. Chairs might need to encourage older faculty to understand that these procedures are necessary to increase the diversity and quality of faculty.

Encourage Mentoring and Integration by Senior Faculty

The willingness of senior faculty to commit to and be involved in the mentoring process is critical to the success of this step of faculty development. It might be helpful to ask faculty to research various mentoring models and to choose the one that fits their departmental culture. If senior faculty view this mentoring role as a means of passing the torch and leaving a legacy, this can become a powerful means of developing faculty and building community in your department. Have senior faculty be the ones to reach out to new faculty, to develop the friendships and collegial activities that will encourage a sense of belonging among newer faculty.

One chair at a state research university organizes the mentoring process at her university this way: "The new probationary faculty members are assigned a mentor by myself and then they get to select one of their own." Allowing the new faculty member to choose one mentor ensures a personality fit in the mentoring experience.

Find ways of recognizing and rewarding senior faculty for these activities. Identify junior faculty who might need special attention, recognizing that minority junior faculty and female faculty might require more time in this process. Create opportunities for collaboration between senior and junior faculty in presentations, papers, and research. Team teaching, coauthoring, and serving on committees are all effective means of enhancing the mentoring process. If there is an ongoing mentoring program for all new faculty, then no one will feel that they are being singled out because of a perceived weakness. You and senior faculty are in the best position to know what is needed. Create the developmental structures and processes for everyone to be successful. The investment will pay dividends over time.

New faculty require the intellectual companionship that comes from interacting with colleagues on campus and elsewhere who share similar interests. One illustration of networking or mentoring comes from a state college with a strong outreach mission. A chair in art and art education first encouraged a new professor to return to graduate school to obtain a doctorate. When the professor earned the credential, the chair began networking with state professional organizations. In speaking of this experience, she explained:

> Having been here so long, I have many contacts. And I have been on many art committees, and when they came around for new people I tried to get this professor on as many of them as possible, especially in the state association. When I stepped aside as president of the association, I appointed him vice president. Now he is president. By my encouraging him to be active in professional organizations, he is now getting a lot of speaking engagements on his own, but initially I gave him contacts.

Visiting with the faculty member involved in this situation confirmed the value to him of this assistance: "She is always encouraging me, giving me information about jobs, placing me on statewide committees—in short, helping me network."

You can foster a climate of trust by creating an open environment where asking questions, seeking and giving feedback, and building relationships is encouraged. This can help new faculty members feel much more welcome and comfortable. It might also give them the opportunity to share their talents and knowledge with seasoned faculty.

Reflecting on what experience had taught him in this regard, a chair at a state university said:

> Always be disposed to be a mentor for newcomers. I think as new departments hire a number of people at the early stages [of career development] it is crucial that they build a sense of trust and collegiality with you early on because I think that sense of relationship comes back to really benefit the department in the long run.

Several institutions, including Kean University, Colorado College, and Temple University, offer new faculty a course reduction in their first semester on campus so that they can participate in mentoring programs. Brigham Young University offers a yearlong orientation for new faculty that includes several luncheons, meetings with mentors, and a two-week learning experience in which new faculty work with each other and senior faculty to develop their own faculty development plan.

Extend Mentoring and Feedback to Graduate Students Who Aspire to be Faculty Members

In graduate institutions, providing many of the same opportunities and support structures for graduate students that are provided for new faculty will help to develop their skills and enhance their contributions to your department and to your academic field. Inviting them to orientations, lectures, explanations of tenure, and informal department gatherings will not require additional preparation or work, but it could increase their motivation and output substantially. Keeping graduate students informed about the labor market, job openings, and teaching/research assistantships and how to apply and interview for these opportunities will increase the likelihood of their success. A chair at a public university who is experimenting with this approach commented that, "For the last three years we've had a monthly department colloquium for discussion of faculty and graduate student work in progress."

Examples of innovative work in this area are sponsored by the Association of American Colleges and Universities and the Council of Graduate Schools. These organizations have developed model programs to better prepare graduate students who are interested in academic careers and have titled their project Preparing Future Faculty.[2] Also, several schools, including Howard University and the University of Minnesota, have developed a curriculum and certification process for graduate students who complete core courses in the area of faculty preparation.

Recognize the Department Chair as a Career Sponsor

A personal commitment to help a newly hired faculty member is a result of several factors. Because chairs are often involved in the hiring process, they hold a personal stake in the long-term career of the individual. As a history chair at a comprehensive college said, "I felt a special responsibility for new faculty coming into the department." Chairs also have a professional responsibility to the academic unit. As another chair commented, "The higher the quality of the faculty, the better the department." Even if you are a new chair who did not hire the faculty member, it is important to communicate your commitment to his or her development. As the department chair, you have the opportunity to contribute in a major way to the career success of a new faculty member. A chair at a Canadian institution put it this way: "I think my job is to facilitate their development and provide direction."

You can make this contribution to their career development through the allocation of resources (e.g., office space, equipment) and by encouraging a collegial environment within the department, one that welcomes new ideas and connects the right mentor to the new faculty member. You also have the ability to assign workloads to allow for transition experiences and to enhance individual talents through the distribution of assignments. You might be able to connect new faculty with senior faculty and resources outside the department, which could provide additional resources and support or collaboration with this new faculty member in teaching or scholarship. Encourage new faculty to attend college-, division-, and institution-wide orientations and developmental workshops. Help them understand the promotion and tenure process and the importance of connecting with other faculty within your department and across the campus.

One chair we interviewed saw career development as one of his most satisfying activities:

> I think one of the most important and certainly one of the most satisfying things that I've done as a chair is to meet toward the end of every semester with every assistant professor for at least an hour—sometimes it's two hours—and to have a serious, frank discussion about the three areas that we use to evaluate people, pretty much the same as elsewhere: scholarship, teaching, and service. I read the course evaluations and I talk with them about what they seem to be doing well and things they might need to work on. I try to give as much practical advice as I can about getting papers accepted at conferences, articles accepted in journals, steps involved in redoing their dissertation as a book, making contacts with publishers, all those sorts of things.

Several schools, including Michigan State University, Colorado State University, and the University of Massachusetts–Amherst, have developed curricula and workshops for chairs that guide them in assisting faculty in their career development. These workshops and guides include ideas for supporting early-career, mid-career, and senior faculty and for rethinking faculty roles and rewards in ways that strengthen and renew departments.

Support Teaching, Particularly at the Undergraduate Level

New faculty should be encouraged to participate in opportunities to improve their teaching. This can be done by sharing course syllabi, providing opportunities to visit the classes of senior faculty, and by providing guides to improve teaching.[3] If at all possible, assign new faculty courses that match their interests, experience, and research. Also, if they have a limited number of course preparations, they will be better able to focus on their teaching. Other information that is helpful to new faculty is the type of student in a course, previous faculty who have taught the course, and the expected preparation, grading time, involvement, and office hours needed. The chair at a state university advises his new faculty that

> one [of the most important tasks] is to improve your skill
> as a teacher using all kinds of means: facilitation, lecture,
> group dynamics, whatever means to improve your teach-
> ing. Not only that, but also introduce more cutting edge
> type of materials for your teaching.

Providing new faculty with funds for equipment, ideas for access to course materials, and necessary tools for research will start them on the track to productivity. As they connect with teaching and learning centers, and find methods of gaining formative feedback, they will find tools for improving their skills and course outcomes. Early supportive feedback from student and colleague evaluations will help direct their future improvement efforts. The more supportive the environment, the more able the new faculty will be to accept and implement constructive comments. Discussions between early-career and senior faculty around teaching and learning issues will also encourage thoughtful growth. Connecting faculty to formal national programs that can assist them as they launch their teaching careers might also be helpful. Lilly Teaching Fellows and Carnegie Scholars Program are two such examples. We continue the discussion of the chair's role in improving teaching performance over the entire course of a faculty member's career in Chapter 6.

Support Scholarly Development

Assigning resources to ensure that pre-tenure faculty receive appropriate support for their research agendas is essential to their long-term success. Basic resources, such as office, lab, and studio space, as well as a computer and support staff, can make a considerable difference to a research program. In this early stage, assuring that travel funds are available for conferences and professional meetings allows new faculty to attend, present papers, develop networking opportunities, and establish a reputation. Encouraging collaboration between senior researchers and new faculty is a great way to spawn new ideas. Formal or informal conversations about ideas in progress might launch creative approaches to writing papers, applying for grants, and new research. Finding alternative approaches to released time allows new faculty additional time to complete research and scholarly projects before their tenure reviews. Developing an integrated view of scholarly work that includes the scholarship of teaching and that responds to community needs and the demand for applied research and public service can also be beneficial. Faculty scholarship is a topic to which we return in Chapter 7.

The chair of a geological sciences department was encouraged about the situation at his state university:

Now there is much more support, much more mentoring that's offered. The provost has instituted annual meetings for nontenured faculty saying here are the things, in a sense, that you need to do to build up your dossier, and here are the things we're going to be looking for, and it's much more supportive. The president comes and speaks at these [meetings] and pretty much says we want you to stay, we've got a lot of money invested in you.

Several schools, including Western Michigan University, the University of California–Davis, the University of Florida, and Indiana University–Bloomington, have set aside funds for pre-tenure faculty use in research and a process for accessing those funds.

Foster a Balance Between Professional and Personal Life

It is important for a department chair to encourage balance in personal and professional life and to model that balance. The chair of a music department at a large state university expressed concern that, "I think the most important thing that I haven't learned how to do yet is to have a rich life outside the college, outside of being a chair." A more satisfied chair from a private university said, "Keep things in perspective. Try to lead a balanced life and try to always have time for yourself, even if you have to schedule it and you know it is hard to step back and look at the big picture and not take things personally."

Techniques of time management that allow for teaching, advising, research, and service are welcomed by anyone, especially a beginning professional. Women and faculty of color might profit from additional support in this area, particularly because they might be in high demand as advisors and as members of institutional committees. As the chair, let faculty know that they can use you as a reason not to take on responsibilities they do not see as priorities or feel pressured to accept. Be an advocate for flexible benefits on your campus that might include wellness programs, child care, part-time status during child-rearing years, and parental leaves. Include information about local community resources as a part of your orientation process. Providing information about schools, child care options, cultural events, recreational opportunities, and events and local attractions helps to encourage this balanced lifestyle. Hosting wellness activities and stress reduction workshops can also help new recruits gain balance in living with the demands of the academic world. Dual career families might also have challenges with finding a job for the spouse. Assistance in these areas can help new faculty members feel supported as they make their transition to your campus.[4]

Conclusion

The next several years will be a period of significant renewal in higher education as a generation of faculty comes to the end of their active careers. In an environment in which many institutions will be competing for new faculty, it will become increasingly important to recruit and retain faculty effectively. The strategies and best practice examples described in this chapter can help chairs to think through the best approach for attracting, socializing, and supporting new faculty so that they are able to reach their potential as contributing professionals.

As the need to consider how to integrate new faculty into your department and help them succeed professionally becomes important to you, you might wish to consider how the following questions can assist your thinking:

- Is my department sufficiently clear in communicating our expectations to new faculty?
- Do we have an effective orientation program that is fully supported by faculty?
- What flexibility do I have to allocate time and funds to new faculty in support of their scholarly endeavors?

- Does our tenure and promotion process provide sufficient opportunities for timely feedback to pre-tenure faculty?

Endnotes

1. The American Association for Higher Education's New Pathways Working Paper Series is intended to stimulate discussion about innovative ways to recast traditional academic practices to accommodate a new generation of scholars and teachers. The authors are indebted to Rice, Sorcinelli, and Austin for ideas they propose in Inquiry #7 in that series.

2. Further information about the Preparing Future Faculty project can be found in the Association of American Colleges and Universities publication, *Building the Faculty We Need: Colleges and Universities Working Together* (Gaff, Pruitt-Logan, & Weibl, 2000).

3. Three excellent resources are Davis's *Tools for Teaching* (1993), McKeachie's *Teaching Tips* (2006), and Bain's *What the Best College Teachers Do* (2004).

4. Several excellent resources are available to campus administrators who are seeking information about innovative work–family policies and practices: *College and University Reference Guide to Work-Family Programs* (Friedman, Rimsky, & Johnson, 1996) and *Work, Family, and the Faculty Career* (Gappa & MacDermid, 1997).

Suggested Resources

Brown, B. E. (2006, September). Supporting and retaining early-career faculty. *Effective Practices for Academic Leaders, 1*(9), 1–16.

   This piece pulls together a range of resources on the development and support of early-career faculty. Considerable research has indicated that it does make a difference to provide this kind of support for success. Numerous strategies are provided, and many other resources are described.

Davis, B. G. (1993). *Tools for teaching.* San Francisco, CA: Jossey-Bass.

   A compendium of classroom teaching strategies and suggestions designed to improve the teaching practices of all college instructors, including beginning, mid-career, and senior faculty members. The book describes 49 teaching tools that cover both traditional, practical tasks—writing a course syllabus, delivering an effective lecture—as well as newer, broader concerns such as responding to diversity on campus and coping with budget constraints.

Gaff, J. G., Pruitt-Logan, A. S., & Weibl, R. A. (2000). *Building the faculty we need: Colleges and universities working together.* Washington, DC: Association of American Colleges and Universities.

This report is a call to change the ways we educate future college professors and a guide for programs that do it. The volume describes what has been accomplished and what has been learned from six years of experience with new faculty preparation programs.

Gappa, J. M., Austin, A. E., & Trice, A. G. (2007). *Rethinking faculty work: Higher education's strategic imperative.* San Francisco, CA: Jossey-Bass.

The authors suggest a need for a strategic approach to faculty work. They trace four major forces affecting higher education institutions. They outline the effects of those changes on faculty, including changing appointments, declining autonomy, escalating work pace, increased entrepreneurial expectations, and conditions of professional development. A useful framework for addressing essential elements of faculty work is developed.

Kouzes, J. M., & Posner, B. Z. (2003). *Jossey-Bass academic administrator's guide to exemplary leadership.* San Francisco, CA: Jossey-Bass.

The core message is "leadership is relationship." The authors indicate that their research has found the characteristics followers most admire in their leaders are: honest, forward looking, competent, and inspiring. Their classic work on the five practices of exemplary leadership is illustrated in a departmental context.

McKeachie, W. J. (1999). *Teaching tips.* Boston, MA: Houghton Mifflin.

This resource is designed as a handbook and provides helpful strategies for dealing with both the everyday problems of teaching at the university level and those that emerge when trying to maximize the learning for all types of students. The recommended strategies are supported by research and grounded in theory.

McKeachie, W. J., & Svinicki, M. (2006). *McKeachie's teaching tips: Strategies, research, and theory for college and university teachers* (12th ed.). Boston, MA: Houghton Mifflin.

This book is designed for faculty as a ready guide for the teaching and learning process. It contains basic how-to information and is a guidebook for teaching at the college and university level. The essentials of course preparation, lecture and laboratory design, testing and assessment, class management and discipline, and writing and research are outlined. The authors also discuss specific details related to teaching college students and bridging the gap between teaching and research.

Rice, R. E., Sorcinelli, M. D., & Austin, A. E. (2000). *Heeding new voices: Academic careers for a new generation* (New Pathways Working Paper Series, Inquiry #7). Washington, DC: American Association for Higher Education.

This paper reports the findings of a yearlong study of structured interviews with new faculty and graduate students aspiring to be faculty members. The study's intent was to give voice to those who are just beginning their academic careers and to provide guidance for senior faculty, chairs, deans, and others in higher education who are responsible for shaping the professoriate.

6

Improve Faculty Teaching

It is easier to encourage someone to become a better scholar than a teacher. Most people coming from graduate school with a Ph.D. know about being a scholar. They often have little knowledge about teaching unless they have a "gift" for it. But even the "gift" needs to be shaped with help, advice, and encouragement.
—*A chair of dance and drama at a liberal arts college*

One of the most important and challenging roles of a department chair is to encourage and support the improvement of teaching. While everyone agrees that teaching is central to the missions of all higher education institutions, the reality is that maintaining a focus on quality of instruction amidst a host of competing demands and interests can be very daunting. The increased specialization of disciplines, ambitious research agendas, the pursuit of grants, and the commercialization of research can seriously divert attention from teaching, especially at the undergraduate level. Nor is the challenge diminished by reward systems that tend in the main to favor research and publication output. Nonetheless, teaching remains an essential component of departmental work, and chairs need to find ways to assist faculty in becoming more effective in the classroom.

The larger the department, the broader the spectrum of teaching-related issues that chairs are likely to have to deal with. The needs of newly hired, first-time teachers will be somewhat different from those who are further along the tenure track. Similarly, these early career faculty will have needs quite different from experienced senior faculty. This chapter, then, provides strategies for promoting quality teaching by all faculty. As you review the methods suggested in the literature on teaching and learning and the recommendations of chairs we interviewed for this handbook, you might wish to reflect on your answers to the following questions:

- Can you recall a particularly effective teacher and what skills and behaviors made the teaching so effective?
- What are some of the ways that you learn best and what are the least effective ways?
- What pedagogies have you had most success using with students?
- What aspects of your teaching have students commented on most favorably?

Promote Excellence in Teaching

Because quality of instruction, like beauty, is often in the eye of the beholder, a good place to start a discussion about improvement is by asking a few basic questions: What is excellence in teaching? How do you know when a teacher is doing an excellent job of facilitating student learning? What outcomes are important in the discipline? What examples of excellence exist on your campus or in your discipline? These are all questions that faculty and students need to consider and understand in order to improve teaching.

Feldman (1988) has studied good teaching both from student and faculty points of view. He found that students want a teacher who provides the following:

- Clarity and organization
- Command of knowledge
- Caring attitude

- Challenge
- Spontaneity
- Drama
- Enthusiasm
- Sincerity
- Acknowledgment
- Sense of humor
- Involvement

This list of attributes and behaviors shows that students value both the technical skills associated with knowledge, clarity, and organization, as well as the relational qualities of caring, enthusiasm, sincerity, sense of humor, and involvement.

The preceding list differs slightly from the list of behaviors that faculty and students both agree should be present in a good teacher. The key traits associated with good teaching and learning on which students and faculty agree are:

- Knowledge of the subject/discipline
- Course preparation and organization
- Clarity and understandability
- Enthusiasm for subject/teaching
- Sensitivity to and concern for students' level and learning progress
- Availability and helpfulness
- Quality of examinations
- Impartiality in evaluation of students' work
- Overall fairness to students

The two lists differ most in the areas of relationship and in drama and spontaneity. Students want to see caring, sincerity, a sense of humor, and involvement, and they enjoy drama and spontaneity. Interestingly, none of these items made it onto the list that both agree should be evident in a good teacher. These traits have much in common with the principles underlying active learning and we recommend this approach as fertile ground for innovative practice and increased student engagement.

An experienced evaluator of faculty teaching performance, Seldin (1994) has identified the basic elements of effective teaching:

> The key ingredients of effective teaching are increasingly known. We have no reason to ignore hundreds of studies that are in general agreement on these characteristics. They include a deep knowledge of the subject, an ability to communicate with and motivate students, enthusiasm for the subject and for teaching, clarity of presentation, and fairness. (p. 3)

Bain (2004) looked at what excellent teachers actually do and reported that the best professors "achieved remarkable success in helping students learn in ways that made a sustained, substantial, and positive influence on how those students think, act, and feel" (p. 5). They changed the thinking of their students in perceptible ways. He adds the follow observation:

> Students developed multiple perspectives and the ability to think about their own thinking; that they tried to understand ideas for themselves; that they attempted to reason with the concepts and information they encountered, to use the material widely, and to relate it to previous experience and learning. (p. 10)

He described the learning of these students as "mind expanding" (p. 5). Bain concludes by suggesting that

> to benefit from what the best teachers do, however, we must embrace a different model, one in which teaching occurs only when the learning takes place. Most fundamentally, teaching in this conception is creating those conditions in which most—if not all—of our students will realize their potential to learn. That sounds like hard work, and it is a little scary because we don't have com-

plete control over who we are, but it is highly rewarding and obtainable. (p. 173)

It is very important to recognize that great teachers are not "born," they are developed. There are professors who have innate abilities that make teaching a more natural skill, but the best teachers are those who, according to Eble (1998), spend considerable amounts of time "conditioning the mind, through acquiring skills, and through practicing amidst intense competition" (cited in Seldin, 1994, p. 1).

Seasoned observers such as Seldin (1993) have witnessed a remarkable increase in the craft of teaching in recent years:

> The interest in improved teaching has mushroomed rapidly in recent years, burrowing into all areas of the country and all types of institutions. Colleges and universities are moving from lip-service endorsements of the importance of teaching to concerted and sustained efforts to improve programs. Faculty and administrators flock to teaching conferences; government agencies and private foundations offer financial support, and a wave of new books on the subject appear. (p. 1)

This renewed interest in teaching is, as Seldin observes, driven as much by external as by internal focus:

> The "new" emphasis on teaching stems from "new" social and political forces. Demographics have changed the student populations and their educational needs. The advent of educational technology has forever altered concepts about teaching and learning. And public outcries demanding accountability have roused legislators and governing boards to actions. All forces rally for improved teaching. (p. 1)

Despite the emphasis on improving teaching, there are several barriers to faculty embracing the idea of improvement wholeheartedly. According to Seldin (1994), these barriers include the following perceptions:

- Many faculty believe that only someone knowledgeable in the discipline can speak meaningfully about the topic or content. They believe that unless a teacher understands the discipline-specific implications of pedagogy, it cannot be applied to their own discipline.
- Many faculty fail to recognize the need for improvement in their own teaching. For example, Blackburn, Bober, O'Donnel, and Pellino (1980) found that 92% believed their own teaching was above average. Follow-up studies by the Carnegie Foundation have found similar results.
- The generic nature of many teaching improvement programs sometimes does not respond to a given teacher's highly personal and specific needs.
- Many faculty have yet to be motivated to cross the threshold of a teaching improvement program. Inertia more than opposition has kept them on the sidelines.

Although there have been many obstacles to teaching improvement, there are also significant developments that encourage the process. They include the major dissatisfaction with the current faculty reward system and the recognition that, if teaching is really valued, it needs to be rewarded accordingly. There is also a growing recognition that today's students are very different from those of the past; they come from more diverse backgrounds; some are older, and many are working full-time while going to school. These students require different teaching methods for learning. There are also societal pressures for improved teaching, including computer technology and telecommunications that have emerged as powerful influences on learning. Distance learning is fast becoming a major vehicle for education, and this mode of communication requires a different set of teaching skills.

Support Teaching Improvement

Given the backdrop of institutional, societal, and technological reasons for improved teaching, how does a chair go about improving the teaching of faculty? Eble and McKeachie (1985) suggest that there are four major approaches that can help as you grapple with this question:

- Enlarging faculty members' knowledge of learning theory and pedagogical practices
- Increasing faculty members' interest in and commitment to teaching
- Reinforcing and rewarding excellent teaching
- Providing opportunities to bring about this kind of growth

Enlarging Faculty Members' Knowledge of Learning Theory and Pedagogical Practices

Expanding awareness of pedagogy can be achieved through a variety of activities that might include workshops reflecting the challenges of a particular discipline; discussion sessions; presentations made by faculty themselves following research on pedagogy; reading clubs; cross-discipline exchanges with other faculty; developing reflective assessment practices as a department, which recognize the culture and understanding of your environment; and creating an environment where continuous improvement in teaching is valued. These activities also encourage faculty to want to understand more about learning theory.

Increasing Faculty Members' Interest in and Commitment to Teaching

The intrinsic reward of seeing the "light come on" in students' eyes and seeing them entertain a new idea for the first time is what motivates many teachers. There is a certain awe in that moment that lights the inner fire of many excellent teachers.

Reinforcing and Rewarding Excellent Teaching

Each of these recommendations is linked to the others. Many professors have a dedication to their discipline, but that dedication might be focused on research more than on teaching. That focus on research can be the result of rewards that are given by the institution and the profession. Careful examination of your department's and institution's reward system might be necessary to understand where faculty are spending their energy and time. Creative chairs find innovative ways to reward outstanding teaching and to reinforce its importance to the department.

Providing Opportunities to Bring About This Kind of Growth

Understanding that faculty have multiple demands on their lives and that they might need opportunities to be reflective about their own teaching can be a gateway to encouraging their growth. Helping teachers to learn from their own teaching experiences can be a great benefit to any professional, and it might be one of the most time-effective means of learning. Teachers might need different kinds of help at different stages in their careers. They also learn differently, just as students do. A wide variety of learning opportunities will assist your efforts. No one method will work for every teacher, so experiment with opportunities and find out what works best for your faculty in their environment and at their career stage.

Many institutions have structures to enhance and improve teaching and learning. They might have different names (teaching and learning centers, academic support centers, instructional support centers), but they often partner with departments to address teaching and learning issues. Departments can use these centers to address many instructional issues as well as tailor their development work to meet the specialized needs of the unit faculty.

In thinking about developing partnerships with your institution-wide effort, keep in mind what the components of successful teaching improvement programs are. Eble and McKeachie (1985), Menges (1991), and Seldin (1993, 1994) suggest the following:

- Tailor the program to the institution's culture.
- Design it for long-term impact but build it for short-term payoffs.
- Structure it with multiple approaches to meet individual preferences, schedules, and styles.
- Gain clear and visible support from top-level administrators and be sure this support is publicly articulated.
- Use advisory groups to design and manage the program.
- Start small and rely on pilot projects that target specific needs or groups.
- Approach the improvement of teaching positively, and offer opportunities for the solid contributors and the stars, not just those who have been ineffective.
- Enable teachers to participate as partners and let them exercise significant autonomy and initiative in shaping their development experiences.
- Enlist substantial numbers of faculty in planning and administering the program.
- Stimulate faculty enthusiasm and a high rate of participation in various aspects of the program. Set up feedback mechanisms to learn of tangible changes in courses, benchmarking strategies, and methodologies or curricula resulting from the program.
- Reduce resistance to the program, not by coercion, but by being willing to listen to others, explain and modify the program, and allow enough time for the program's acceptance.
- Recognize and reward excellence in teaching.

Address Teaching Problems

The preceding suggestions are helpful when developing a teaching improvement program for your department and ensuring that the institution-wide effort addresses instructional priorities. But what do you do when faculty members are not performing to the best of their abilities? How do you handle student complaints about a faculty member who is not doing a good job? Where is the line between improving performance and evaluating current performance? These are real issues that every academic chair will encounter. Because department chairs often evaluate faculty and provide rewards for good teaching, they can be instrumental in offering assistance to professors whose performance is unacceptable. In this chapter we suggest a five-step process for improving teaching performance based largely on the consultative models available from the field of instructional development.

Even though the line between development and evaluation is sometimes difficult to draw, the following five guidelines are based on the assumption that, as the chair, you are focused on helping to improve the teaching performance of faculty.

Gather Background Information

Before visiting individually with a faculty member about teaching problems, the chair should gather information about the individual's performance. Be sure to utilize as many sources as possible to gain this understanding. Student evaluations are one source of information, but they are not the only way to understand what is happening in a classroom. Visit with students in your office, talk with senior faculty and administrators, check records in your personnel files to see if there are previous complaints or compliments about a specific teacher. Look for behavioral signs of problems. The signs might be on the faces of the individuals or in their voices as they mention their concerns. "I noticed that he was flustered and found it very difficult to teach. He brought this concern to me," said the chair of an English department at a selective liberal arts college. The signs might be even more overt, as in the case of the faculty member who "would frequently tape a sign on the door that said 'No Class Today.'"

Clarify Goals and Objectives

After gathering information about a potential teaching problem, visit with the faculty member formally (e.g., a scheduled meeting in the faculty member's office) at the earliest possible opportunity. If a semiannual or annual performance review is due, set aside time during this review to talk about the growth and development of the faculty member as a teacher. For example, at a research university department with 18 faculty, the fine arts chair "interviewed all faculty members every semester, giving them an opportunity to present their concerns to me (and giving me one to present my concerns to them)." A business chair at a comprehensive college meets with faculty at the beginning of each academic year. In this interview, the faculty member is asked to share two personal and professional goals, and the chair does the same. In this way they share and agree upon goals for the year. Both beginning-of-year and end-of-year sessions provide an opportunity to explore and clarify teaching problems with faculty.

Lewis (1988) calls this phase "conducting a pre-observation interview." The first step is to review how the faculty member feels about the courses, students, teaching, and causes of the potential problem:

- Ask for a description of his or her class(es) verbally as well as through the syllabus for the course.
- Listen for indications of the specific types of feedback the faculty member is seeking or needs (e.g., "Are my lectures organized?" "Am I responding adequately to students' questions?").

- Pay attention to comments that reflect the faculty member's attitude toward students and teaching.
- Ask if there are any personal factors that might be affecting his or her professional activities (e.g., a new baby or overcommitment on committees).

Second, attempt to discern the issues involved, taking into consideration the experience level of the faculty member in question. Exemplary chairs in our study mentioned that the problem of inexperienced teachers often relates to adjusting to students and the classroom setting and learning the student evaluation procedure. For example, the problems of inexperienced teachers include:

- Inadequate speaking and communication skills in the classroom
- Unfair grading practices
- More interest in research than in teaching and students
- Inability to relate appropriately to the knowledge level of students
- Unfamiliarity with administering student evaluation forms and interpreting results from them

The problems of experienced teachers often manifest themselves in different ways:

- Dry, unstimulating lecture methods or a "drab" personality
- An arrogant, condescending approach to communication with students
- Lack of updated materials and research in classroom content
- Inconsistent and disorganized instructional practices, such as changing times when tests are given, changing assignments, and not paying attention to the syllabus

Third, find out how the individual sees the situation. Some might not be aware of a problem; others might be suffering through a painful experience. Regardless of the case, finding out how the individual views the situation can clarify the problem and demonstrate respect for his or her views. Use good interpersonal skills, such as active listening and feedback, that were introduced in Chapter 4. "Don't be afraid to confront the individual," said one chair, and "realize that he may not be aware of the problem, especially in the case of senior, experienced faculty." Understand, too, that when you are dealing with senior faculty who are experiencing difficulties with their teaching, you might be dealing with an accumulation of habitual practice that is difficult to change. The chair of a humanities department at a small liberal arts college put the challenge quite directly: "How do you change the personality of a faculty member who has been teaching for 25 years?"

This point was brought home in an illustration about a disorganized teacher, a 45-year-old tenured faculty member in a humanities department at a liberal arts institution who continually changed assignments, requirements, and test dates. After students complained, the chair visited with her and reported this reaction: "At first she seemed shocked that there was a problem. She wasn't aware of it. After the shock wore off, she seemed resentful for a while and avoided me whenever she could." In approaching a difficult case such as this, a chair might follow these steps:

- Start easy; she needs a friend. Work on the problem together and talk in a nonthreatening way.
- Explore with her the specific source of her disorganization. Why is she disorganized?
- Suggest alternatives to her that will present new challenges. Help her find developmental grant money.
- Consider team teaching with her or assign someone who would be willing to team teach with her.
- Refer her to a faculty development program or center if one exists on campus or use an Internet site as a resource for improvement in a specific area.

Observe the Performance Yourself

Your objective at this point is to explore further the potential problem of the individual so that an appropriate improvement plan can be developed. Consider observing this faculty member teaching a class, particularly one that focuses on the specific issues in question. Peer review involving others in the department is also an option, but experts indicate that a formalized process with training and multiple visits is most effective and reliable. This might be a useful system for a department to embark on as a developmental strategy.

One faculty member had difficulty as a teacher because he spoke above the knowledge level of the students. A chair in biology talked about visiting this individual's classroom:

> I sat in on his class and tried to analyze what the problem might be and later tried to point out difficulties he experienced in conveying information from a basic, lower level of understanding to more complex thoughts. We talked about the thought process of poorly prepared students.

As this comment indicates, the chair visited with the individual about areas of difficulty after observing his classroom performance, and he could then draw on his experience to facilitate understanding of the issue.

Observing performance will be more objective and might be less obtrusive through use of videotape. A chemistry chairperson at a small liberal arts college described the use of videotaping as a vehicle for sharing information about good teaching techniques: "We set up a program where he would videotape his lectures and I would videotape my lectures, and we would talk about what I was doing and what he was doing. It was a mechanism to see myself." Taylor-Way (1988) recommends a videotape recall method for improving teaching. A teacher videotapes the first 20 minutes of a class. The chair reviews the tape with the faculty member within 24 hours while the teacher's memory of the class is reasonably fresh. The videotape is interrupted periodically for the teacher to discuss how she or he feels, thinks, and acts in teaching during the segment. Then the chair uses a three-step process:

- Focus on a specific, discrete pattern or regularity where there is a discrepancy between what the teacher sees on the videotape and a more preferred approach.
- Give a name to that pattern or regularity.
- Reframe or develop with the teacher a strategy or principle for reducing the discrepancy. The objective here is to encourage the teacher to add to his or her repertoire of options.

Facilitate Improvement and the Practice of New Skills

Work with the individual to develop a plan for improvement. This plan might evolve from sharing information about teaching tips found in books, articles, workshops, or online. "We have a large bulletin board in the hall," said one chairperson, "where I post notices about upcoming seminars or campus activities that relate to teaching." Refer "problem" teachers to development committees or instructional development centers where they can access assistance in diagnosing problems and in observing classroom techniques. An accounting chair at a research university routinely referred inexperienced faculty to such a center. He explained:

> I visited with a junior faculty member and pointed out certain teaching problems. This person was shocked that teaching evaluations were not up to the level he had received at another institution. I suggested he get in touch with the campus office of instructional development. People from that office came over, talked with him, went to his class, and they videotaped one of his classes. Also, they helped him rework the way he pre-

pared for class and how he conducted the class. As a result, he felt much better about his teaching.

Chairs can provide more experienced faculty with material that is useful for course content. A tenured faculty member who had spent 16 years in a life sciences department is seen as a "willing soul: She is willing to pitch in and do whatever is asked of her, and she has a deep commitment to the department. But she had problems delivering clear instructions to students, planning for instruction, and including current research in her courses." She had attended at least 10 professional conferences, but she did not seem to be able to apply that information in her classes. The chair described the assistance provided:

> I made available to her some literature in her subject field by subscribing to journals that were not in our library. These journals would come directly to her. In addition, I have had several individual conferences with her and we have talked about ways to include current research in our lectures.

The chair need not be solely responsible for sharing information with faculty. A business college at a major university used outside experts to assist one faculty member in keeping current and credible in an area "where the content and technology were moving so fast that faculty just couldn't keep up." The college brought in outside people from business and industry to address current topics. The outside expertise added credibility to the faculty member's class, and the professor learned a lot about activities in the field.

Practicing elements of good teaching is an important step toward improvement. Exemplary chairs we interviewed served as mentors for faculty and role modeled good teaching behaviors with faculty. For example, a chairperson of English at a liberal arts college recommended to an inexperienced teacher that he attend the chair's class as well as the class of a senior faculty member:

My assistance involved a number of long conversations, and I invited him to sit in on my own classes. At least one other senior member has had him sit in on his classes as well. I should add that this man has been reappointed, and while his problems have not been resolved in the classroom, I think he's certainly improved a great deal and that he feels the department is on his side.

Chairs can also share their approaches through a team-teaching situation or working directly with the faculty member on the development of course syllabi or course content.

Monitor Progress and Advocate for the Individual

At this point in the process, you should begin to cycle back to the first step of gathering information, only this time you review materials and information about a specific problem or issue to determine whether the individual is making progress. This monitoring process takes time: reviewing semester and annual student evaluation forms, visiting with students, and learning from colleagues as well as the individual faculty member.

When improvement occurs, consider your role as that of an advocate for the faculty member with those responsible on campus for evaluating and assessing performance. A chair at a liberal arts institution talked about this step:

> After the person's work began to show some signs of improvement, I told members of the evaluation committee and other members in the department to spread the good word that he was trying to improve his teaching and we had evidence in hand.

This is only effective if you honestly and sincerely believe that the individual's performance is improving and that it has a good possibility of meeting expectations for promotion. If it is evident that things are not improving and are not likely to improve even with further help, the chair should communicate this assessment. You cannot know beforehand whether your faculty will improve sufficiently to be promoted, tenured, or meet another's expectations for performance. It also means having to deal with your own feelings of potential failure. You can only *try* to help someone in your department to improve his or her performance. Ultimately, it is up to the individual to achieve the performance standards set by the department.

Employ Case Studies to Guide Your Response to Teaching Problems

We will illustrate the process of improving teaching performance with two specific cases. Both are drawn from small liberal arts colleges where a major emphasis is placed on good teaching. The first situation involved a new, untenured professor who joined the staff in the education department. The individual possessed excellent writing and research skills, but she needed to improve her teaching. "She was a sit-down teacher, and she had difficulty conveying information students could relate to." The chairperson described the following steps:

- Gathering background information: During the first year the chair "just spent time sitting in her office, talking to her, and not doing much." However, the chair also visited with students about complaints and carefully reviewed the students' evaluations.
- Clarifying the problem: By the end of the second year, it was necessary to begin taking steps to improve the individual's teaching. The chair and the faculty member met and began thinking about a "faculty development plan." Several activities were carried out under this plan.

- Observing performance yourself: The chair videotaped the faculty member's teaching in a couple of classes and then reviewed the individual's strengths and weaknesses as a teacher. Together they isolated teaching behaviors that needed improvement. The chair sat in on a couple of her classes to observe her teaching.
- Facilitating improvement and practice: They team taught a course together. This class required that both the chair and the faculty member attend every session. Finally, the dean provided a summer faculty development grant so that the chair and the faculty member could spend three weeks during the summer modifying one of her courses.
- Monitoring progress: Over a period of several years, the chair monitored student evaluations. By the sixth year, teaching had improved: "She had gone from approximately 1.5 on a 5-point scale (5 as the high point) to 4.1 or 4.2 in the intervening years." At the end of her sixth year, she was given tenure.

The second case involved a tenured faculty member in a speech area at a small liberal arts college. This person was an assistant professor who wanted to be promoted to associate professor. Five years earlier the faculty member had gone up for promotion and was denied; now he wrote to the chair requesting that his credentials be reviewed once again. Here is how the chair used the process to respond to the faculty member's issue:

- Gathering background information: The chair went to the faculty member to get his permission to study the recommendations of the previous promotion and tenure committee. He indicated that, "I'm reluctant to tell people what to do unless the situation calls for it and they will welcome such help." Then he talked with each member of the department to compile a description of what the individual should do to improve his teaching.

- Clarifying the problem: Next the chair visited with the faculty member about what needed to be done. He asked, "What kind of response do you want from students? Are you interested in finding out what you need to do to improve?"

- Observing performance: The chair suggested that senior faculty members attend the individual's classes and make suggestions for improvement. He adopted a gentle approach because "You've just got to ease the person along. See what you can do."

- Advocating on behalf of the individual: While the individual worked on improving his teaching, the chair told the provost that the person "is working on his teaching." The chair also told members of the promotion committee about the person's progress.

These cases illustrate ways in which the strategies discussed in this chapter can be put into practice in quite specific circumstances.

Conclusion

If we accept Bain's (2004) definition, we will understand that excellent teaching takes place when learning occurs. Excellent teaching is a "mind expanding" experience that allows students to develop "multiple perspectives and the ability to think about their own thinking; to understand ideas for themselves; to attempt to reason with the concepts and information they encounter; to use the material widely; and to relate it to previous experience and learning" (p. 10). It is the department chair who has the greatest opportunity to influence improvement in teaching through expanding faculty knowledge of pedagogy, increasing interest in teaching, reinforcing and rewarding excellent teaching, and providing opportunities for growth. The five-step process for improving faculty teaching performance, which is outlined in this chapter, can be adapted to most departmental circumstances.

In thinking about the future of teaching in your department, here are some questions that might provide some guidance:

- What can we do in our department to encourage a high priority on teaching?
- What can we do to develop a culture of improvement?
- How are we preparing for innovations in teaching and technology?
- What are we doing to become familiar with the students of the future—their interests and learning styles?
- How is our department employing the teaching resources on campus?
- Who can provide instructional leadership in the department?

Suggested Resources

Bain, K. (2004). *What the best college teachers do*. Cambridge, MA: Harvard University Press.

　　Bain provides insight into what more than 100 highly effective teachers do to increase student learning. Students suggest that these instructors opened "windows on the world" or new ways to think about issues. If education and learning are about change in thinking and behavior, then this book provides valuable perspective and strategy.

Bland, C. J., & Risbey, K. R. (2006, July). Faculty development programs. *Effective Practices for Academic Leaders*, 1(7), 1–16.

　　The authors provide an overview of the background of faculty development and identify issues over the faculty career span—new, mid-career, late stage, and retirement. Emphasis is placed particularly on teaching and research. The publication contains frameworks and strategies to develop programs and activities.

Davis, B. G. (1993). *Tools for teaching*. San Francisco, CA: Jossey-Bass.

　　A compendium of classroom-tested strategies and suggestions designed to improve the teaching practices of all college instructors, including beginning, mid-career, and senior faculty members. The book describes 49 teaching tools that cover both traditional, practical tasks—writing a course syllabus, delivering an effective lecture—as well as newer, broader concerns such as responding to diversity on campus and coping with budget constraints.

McKeachie, W. J., & Svinicki, M. (2006). *McKeachie's teaching tips: Strategies, research, and theory for college and university teachers* (12th ed.). Boston, MA: Houghton Mifflin.

Originally written for beginning teachers, this is a classic work in terms of providing a faculty member with information and strategies to address the host of teaching issues they are likely to face. Now in its 12th edition, it has been expanded to address virtual as well as face-to-face classrooms. Whether it is organizing content, devising tests, addressing cheating, grading, or most anything that a teacher can imagine, this book has many valuable suggestions.

7

Improve the Scholarship of Faculty

The highly research-productive department is a carefully constructed mosaic of individual, environmental, and leadership features. When this mosaic is developed and continually nurtured, the result is synergistic—it creates a research-conducive organization that is more than a sum of its parts, and it yields researchers who are better (i.e., more productive) than they would be elsewhere.
—Bland, Weber-Main, Lund, and Finstad, 2005

The classic image of a professor is someone who generates new knowledge as well as disseminates knowledge through writing and professing. Through research, the creation of new knowledge has long been rewarded and emphasized at major research universities, and publications and scholarly work are assuming a more central role in the working lives of faculty at comprehensive universities as well as at liberal arts institutions. In light of this fact, faculty need to perform capably on all college campuses as scholars as well as teachers.

For both the department and its chair, answering the following questions can help to ensure that faculty understand what is expected and what is included in scholarship: Where do traditional research and other forms of scholarly activity fit into the expectations of being a faculty member? Are creative activities such as those in the humanities included? What is the working definition used in the department? How are expectations communicated and reinforced? Some departments range from basic and applied research to creation of artistic products. Others might apply more narrow definitions. Whatever the situation, it is important to develop an understanding of what is expected and accepted as scholarship in the department.

Many institutions and departments have found Boyer's work in *Scholarship Reconsidered* (1990) to be quite useful. In addition to the traditional scholarship of discovery (contributing to the stock of human knowledge), Boyer identifies three important forms for scholarship: integration—synthesizing and integrating knowledge; application—putting knowledge into action through professional practice; and teaching—transforming and extending knowledge through teaching. This model suggests that research, teaching, and service can all have their scholarly focus. Some institutions and departments have made all four forms of scholarship part of their promotion and tenure criteria. O'Meara and Rice (2005) provide an in-depth look at the four types of scholarship and how a range of institutions have incorporated them. Their examples suggest that moving from commitment to implementation has its challenges. Deciding on the nature of scholarship is critical to any kind of promotion and improvement process so that faculty members will be recognized and rewarded for their efforts.

Foster a Strong Research Climate

For those institutions that focus on the more traditional forms of research, keys to productivity have been identified. In a literature review combined with an in-depth study of a major research institution, Bland, Weber-Main, Lund, and Finstad (2005) indicate that there are three overarching aspects to successful departmental research performance: individual, institutional, and leadership characteristics. These features suggest that to have high research productivity requires strong individual research socialization, a clear institutional focus, and leadership/peer reinforcement. In highly focused research institutions, these factors are well aligned.

The work of Bland et al. (2005) also suggests that if a strong research climate is desired, there are proven strategies to implement productivity. For those institutions with a more multifaceted mission or primarily a teaching focus, the pathway might not be so clear. Chairs have often voiced a concern in times of decreasing funding that faculty must find outside resources to support their scholarly activities, an expectation that some faculty do not see as their responsibility. As every administrator knows, these activities also generate overhead revenue that is prized by the institution to offset institutional costs and provide flexibility. Beyond what constitutes scholarship, department chairs must decide if it is worth the time and effort to attempt to improve scholarship both on a department and individual level.

At a department level, Bland et al. (2005, pp. 12–13) suggest that there are institutional strategies that can be utilized to increase the research culture. These include clear goals that coordinate work and emphasize research; shared culture and positive climate; mentoring; communication with colleagues—professional networks; interdisciplinary collaboration; resources; teaching; sufficient time for research; rewards; brokered opportunity structure; faculty size and diversity; and leadership and governance—both of the chair and the faculty. However, as Bland and her colleagues note, the process begins with selection and recruitment. They suggest that if the individual is properly socialized in graduate school, then the person will have the attitude, skills, and some experience in understanding and embracing the lifestyle needed for research. Specifically, they indicate that the following individual characteristics are necessary: strong motivation to conduct research; demonstrated research experience; good fit between the candidate and the department; ability to collaborate; highest standard of excellence; and strong teaching skills (p. 21). In some cases, the chair might not be able to change the conditions identified for highly effective research departments (e.g., faculty size and diversity), so then the question becomes what is the minimum number or how can a critical mass be achieved? If this threshold cannot be met within the department, then other strategies such as collaborating with faculty in other departments and institutions to build the needed cluster might be required.

Many of the books and workshops for new faculty suggest that they need to be shielded from time-consuming activities (i.e., advising, teaching large classes, committee work) so that they can establish their research. It is also suggested that the chair and other faculty mentor the new faculty member both in priorities and time management as well as in the specific function of research.

A question a chair needs to address with individuals without a research focus is: Might it be more productive to have differentiated contributions in which people who are not skilled or interested in research concentrate on other duties such as teaching, advising, and service? At least the department gains other important functions that the faculty member enjoys and is effective in doing. A department chair of physics at a doctoral-level institution indicated that, "I am a firm believer that the chair should as much as possible lead by example in terms of trying to do the best job in teaching and maintaining an active research program."

Wergin (2003) has provided a process for departments to look at assessing quality from an inside-out perspective. In other words, the department can determine what is important, in this case scholarship, and then describe and provide the necessary processes and performance criteria to be successful in these endeavors.

Many, if not most, faculty who are early in their careers initiate, maintain, and focus on a line of scholarly inquiry. When this fails to happen, especially by the third or fourth year, they jeopardize their chances of being promoted or tenured. When tenured faculty have inadequate research portfolios, they risk a negative review for promotion to full professor or become perceived as noncontributing members in departments. Some tenured faculty hired years ago as teachers, not researchers, might need to reallocate efforts into scholarly activities, learn the skills of a researcher, and engage in a modicum of scholarly work. The chair of an agricultural department at a research university commented:

> I don't believe there is a faculty member who doesn't want to be productive. Everyone wants to be. I don't believe there is a faculty member who can't be productive as long as you can find an area where he or she can contribute.

The chair of a physical education department at a regional university puts the issue this way: "I think they were at a plateau. All they needed was a little spark. I think I know their potential. And I've devised that little spark they needed to get them actively involved in research."

When faced with "problem" faculty who need to improve their research performance, how can chairs help? In this chapter we advance a four-step model based on interviews with exemplary chairs who spoke about improving the research of their faculty:

- Detect a problem situation as early as possible by having a review process in place.
- When you detect a problem, visit with the individual to clarify the nature and reasons for it.
- Identify a plan for improvement that incorporates strategies within your control.
- After a suitable period of time, follow up on the plan to see if it has had a positive impact on the individual's behavior; if so, advocate for the individual with faculty and administrators.

Detect a Problem Situation as Early as Possible

A performance discrepancy, according to Mager and Pipe (1970), is a difference between "someone's actual performance and his (or her) desired performance" (p. 7). Feedback about performance discrepancies can come from promotion and tenure committee members, faculty colleagues, students, administrators, or your own subjective assessment of the situation. The potential problem should be detected as early as possible. This means that a careful review of performance for untenured faculty should be conducted by at least their third year, well in advance of their tenure review. As a communications chair at a doctoral-granting school said, "It's important to catch problems early because it's impossible to help someone in their fourth or fifth year." For tenured faculty, a process of annual review is helpful because research performance can wax and wane during a career. As mentioned in Chapter 3, a faculty performance information system in the department is a useful mechanism for monitoring faculty output.

Annual performance reviews have become a well-accepted procedure on college campuses. These reviews, conducted at the conclusion of an academic year, provide an opportunity for chairs to regularly assess the research productivity of their faculty. Curry (2006), a well-known writer on faculty evaluation procedures, offers the following advice about annual academic performance reviews:

> At a minimum, performance appraisal or review is related to a process of comparing performance to standards and providing feedback to the faculty member about that performance. More fully, the performance review process begins with identification and enunciation of institutional goals, vision and values and with the unit establishment of equitable unit workloads, performance criteria and standards. (p. 3)

A more elaborate model might include a modified management-by-objective approach whereby goals mutually agreed upon by the chair and faculty member and specified at the beginning of the academic year are compared with the accomplishments at the end of the year. Faculty might organize information for the chair to review prior to the meeting. The level and type of detailed documentation required in this type of review will vary. However, it can include:

- *Quantitative measures* such as number of papers presented at conferences, journal articles published, books written, grant proposals authored or funded, and creative performances given.
- *Qualitative measures* such as citations in published works, articles in high-quality journals, success rate of proposals for research support, attendance at performances, or positive reviews of performances.
- *Peer judgments* such as letters of support by peers on and off campus and department chair and dean comments.
- *Eminence measures* such as editorial board appointments to journals, awards for research from professional organizations, invited papers, or requested performances.
- *Self-evaluations* such as personal statements about performance.

Many institutions now have a set of quality indicators for research that are used to compare faculty both within the department and across the institution as well as to peer institutional faculty. These factors are used as the baseline for assessing rankings and determining progress in ranking.

In addition to the types of documentation previously listed, faculty might be asked to answer a set of questions related to their research agendas: What impact has their scholarly work had on individuals and groups off campus? What thread of continuity exists among the works? What resources are needed to better conduct scholarly work? How is the work original or unique? What is the individual's plan for continued growth as a researcher?

Annual achievement reports of scholarly performance can be promoted by chairs in a unit. One such report became a mechanism for motivating senior faculty in a philosophy department. A specially appointed faculty performance committee in that department collected research data from faculty and organized it into a report. This report contained information about faculty accomplishments during the year and anticipated accomplishments during the next year. In the process of compiling the report, the committee resolved difficult questions such as: What are the major areas of research productivity? How do we weigh them? How do we determine that one person's performance is better than another's? "As a result," commented the chair, "the faculty get to see a cross-section of all of their colleagues. It heightens their awareness of their own productivity, and it encourages them to plan."

An informal review system might work equally well. Chairs can visit informally with faculty about their performance, asking them about progress, new ventures, and their hopes for publications. This practice seems to work with senior faculty, as a computer science chair at a major research university observed: "He'd come in and I would say, 'How's it going? How is your book coming along?' You know, it's all those little things."

Clarify the Reasons for Lack of Performance

Explore with the faculty member the nature of the problem and the reasons for it. Keep in mind the importance of the process; be mindful of the good listening skills and appropriate feedback approaches mentioned in Chapter 4 of this book. For example, make the individual feel comfortable (an active listening skill) and give feedback when the individual is ready for it (a feedback skill). A veterinary science chair talked about his process:

It is difficult when you're dealing with criticism and at the same time providing total support for an individual.

> When you visit with a person, after you break the ice and introduce the problem as you see it, you might say, "Now that probably looks negative to you, but it is my responsibility to try to address this situation, turn it around, look at the positive side, and see what we can do."

The individual might deny the problem at first or become enraged or angered, similar to the first steps in the grieving or dying process, which has been well documented by Elizabeth Kübler-Ross.[1] This initial reaction should, with support and understanding, give way to acceptance and a willingness to explore or seek options for improving performance. In some cases, the process can be conducted within a single meeting; in others it might require a series of discussions.

During these visits, explore the reasons or causes for poor research performance. At least four types of causes surfaced during our interviews, and they illustrate the range of possibilities.[2]

1. *Lack of skills*

   • Lacks effective research skills such as computer, writing, library, or method skills.

   • Needs to improve skills in a specific scholarly area such as learning to write grant proposals or learning to combine artistic performances with writing.

2. *Lack of motivation and interest*

   • Spends an inordinate amount of time on teaching duties and claims not to have time for research.

   • Devotes virtually the entire time to training students and considers undergraduate teaching and what happens to students after graduation to be the ultimate priorities.

3. *Personal reasons*

   • Lacks patience necessary to revise and improve manuscripts.

- Holds standards so high that all research is imperfect (a clue: manuscripts are labeled "draft").

- Interests keep shifting; person dabbles in many areas, causing unfocused research.

- Takes a rejection notice from a publisher or editorial board as a bitter defeat and vows not to write again.

4. *Obstacles in the work setting*

- Lacks the equipment necessary to conduct research.

- Has too many assignments unrelated to research so that time is not available to conduct scholarly work.

- Works in an area in which external funds are not available for scholarly research.

These are but a few of the reasons that might surface in your conversations with a faculty member. It is helpful to understand them if you are to develop a cooperative plan for improving performance.

Identify a Plan for Improvement

A plan for improvement should incorporate activities and resources at your command as well as those available from the individual you are helping. Our discussion will be focused on strategies that chairs can use to intervene in an unproductive research situation. You might wish to consider these two ideas. First, use multiple strategies rather than limiting yourself to one. For example, a communications chair in a doctoral-granting institution used the following process with an older assistant professor who had 10 years of professional experience before going back for a Ph.D.:

- He visited with the individual about areas of interest.
- He talked with individuals in the field and called them to discuss the faculty member's research interests.
- He encouraged the person to publish from her dissertation.

- He contacted individuals in her professional association about the possibility of presenting her research at a national conference.
- He worked with the person to discuss how to rewrite conference papers into journal articles and how to identify appropriate journals in the field for publication.

One sentence summarized the situation for this chair: "We began to get the person into the research process—thinking about things, doing some research, writing papers, going to national meetings, and taking feedback and turning it into publications."

Second, individualize the improvement plan. Assess whether the plan is consistent with the needs of individuals at their career stage. The approach needs to differ for senior as opposed to junior faculty. Senior faculty require less obtrusive, more subtle and indirect approaches than junior faculty. Practices such as encouraging, supporting, praising, appreciating, and matching interests with resources are more facilitating strategies for senior faculty than junior faculty. For junior faculty, the approach can be more direct and might include talking with them about your perceptions of their needs and then establishing a plan of activities, including such components as allocating resources, representing the individual, role modeling and mentoring, and supporting and encouraging the beginning researcher.

Allocating resources. Chairs can support faculty, especially junior faculty, by adjusting workloads and assignments, allocating funds, providing information, and finding research equipment. The chair of an accounting department at a research university commented about adjusting workloads:

> I work in the direction of providing released time for research. I've reduced the teaching loads of all faculty so they only teach two classes a quarter and hopefully not more than four preparations during the year. I give faculty released time when they have research projects.

Funds and support services are important in helping untenured faculty members improve their performance. Resources under a chair's control often include secretarial assistance, research leaves, travel to professional meetings to present papers, and graduate assistants. An engineering chair at a doctoral-granting school described the resources needed by one untenured faculty member:

> An assistant professor right out of school joined the department. The real problem was how to help him get started in the fastest way. I got him involved in our graduate program so that he would have graduate research assistants. I got him some internal support, some equipment and money. Finally, I assisted him in getting a foundation award of $60,000 over a three-year period for his own development. All of this gave him a base of support from which to operate and from which to get started.

A tenured faculty member who had "two or three good papers very early in his career went through a 15-year dry spell in publishing and didn't write because he had too high standards." His helper, a chair in a social sciences department, provided rewards for publishing: "I took a 'no-nonsense' approach to rewards: I gave him a big salary raise. When he published something, it was extremely good. I saw to it that he received rewards for his research." Another individual in a music department with a half-time academic appointment and a half-time performing arts position received information from the chair about expectations for achieving tenure:

> I identified what I thought the issues were and set up a series of meetings with the dean and with other faculty to talk about the criteria for evaluation. After that I visited with the faculty member about a five-year schedule of research, performance, and teaching, and talked about his schedule to make his research time most productive.

These examples illustrate practices associated with reducing teaching loads, providing start-up and equipment funds, and clarifying expectations for evaluation, all of which are examples of allocating the resources of assignment, funds, and information.

Representing the individual. Chairs can help faculty improve their performance by representing them (or advocating for them) to other individuals. You can negotiate with the dean for reduced loads and assignments and forward information to deans about the research progress of individuals. Especially for untenured faculty, chairs can network with researchers and scholars both on and off campus to assist the individual. They can put faculty in touch with conference planners and funding agencies. A fine arts chair discussed a faculty member who "did not have a research record that would merit tenure." This individual had professional experience outside the academy prior to his doctoral program but he "had difficulty translating experiences into professional research activities." What did the chair do? He visited with him about research interests and then "called individuals on other campuses and put the person in touch with researchers."

Representing individuals on campus provides visibility for their accomplishments. It also leads to important recognition of accomplishments, which is a strong motivator for individuals to continue producing scholarly works. A finance chair believed in letting others know about the quality of work in the "pipeline":

> People aren't really on top of what is going on—they only evaluate what is published, not the work in the pipeline. My problem has been to communicate that the work in progress is good and going to be published.

One approach to visibility is to place the individual on important committees so that the person gets to know other faculty. One chair commented:

> I've given him good committee assignments that are easy and of high visibility so that he can have a good

track record for promotion. While he waits for his articles to come through, he looks good to faculty and
administrators.

Role modeling and mentoring. You can facilitate the research of
faculty by collaborating with them on projects and by reviewing
and providing feedback on their manuscripts and projects. This
idea is reinforced by Bland et al. (2005): "A summative message
that emerges from this body of research is that mentoring, when
done well, can have a wide-reaching, positive impact on the
research productivity of faculty" (p. 66). Chairs mentor and share
their expertise with untenured faculty by collaborating with them
in finding research funds, in selecting general research topics, and
in teaming on projects. One chair reinforced the value of such
joint projects: "We worked on collaborative projects. This means
involving them in some of my research projects and then making
it clear that they need to get their own projects going later on, on
their own initiative."

A chair was able to encourage an assistant professor in physical
education by coupling the faculty member's interests with the assistant professor's coaching interests. Because the scholarly interests
of the individual were in the same areas as the chair's, they began
collaborating on research. They created a questionnaire, distributed
it, analyzed the results, and wrote up the findings. Soon afterward,
the faculty member reported the research at a regional conference.
Since then, conference coordinators have asked the faculty member to present other research papers. Now she is saying, "This is
really great. When can we get ready for next year?"

Collaboration might mean that the chair reacts to faculty grant
proposals. An engineering chair at a doctoral-granting institution
talked about a second-year faculty member who didn't know how
to write a grant proposal. In this case, when the individual produced
a proposal, the chair provided a thorough review and critique:

I've spent 15 to 16 years in academia watching talented
new Ph.D.s get "ground up" by the system. Some people

have the ability to conduct research, but they haven't learned the art of grantsmanship. They lack skills in selling their ideas.

For one second-year faculty member, I reviewed all his proposals and worked on format and budget. I don't really tell him what kind of research to do because he's not working in my area, but I'm a fairly experienced proposal evaluator. I can read his proposal and tell him whether it's going to hold the interest of the potential funding agency.

Often faculty struggle to understand editors' criticisms and comments on manuscripts. Helping faculty interpret editorial comments on manuscripts is an important form of assistance. A chair in a family and human resources department talked about junior faculty being "ravaged" by editorial reviews:

When junior faculty submit a manuscript to a respectable and competitive journal and the manuscript comes back "ravaged" by the reviewer, the novice researcher says: "This is the poorest manuscript that they have ever received." A negative review, however slight, can crush a new faculty member who has put in a tremendous amount of time on the paper. The chair needs to help the junior faculty member understand that such a review is typical, and unless the paper is ruled out completely, to revise, revise, and revise.

By reviewing comments from reviewers, by reacting to papers and proposals, and by working directly with the individual on research projects, the chair supports the continued research improvement of a faculty member.

Supporting and encouraging. A final set of practices for supporting faculty involves discovering a faculty member's interests and matching them with resources, as well as appreciating and acknowledging a faculty member's scholarly work. For example, a chair in special education at a major university described a tenured faculty member who had no professional publications during a two- to three-year period. The chair explained, "Few attempts had been made to write grants. Each had resulted in dismal failure." Commenting on this situation, the chair remarked, "I first identified the interests of the individual, linked resources to his interests, and made myself an integral player, as a good colleague or role model, in facilitating his efforts."

The chairs we interviewed spoke often about stressing individual strengths: appreciating an individual's work and providing encouragement and praise. A psychology chair at a doctoral-granting institution sought to create a better research atmosphere in his department where "they all had good teaching evaluations, but none of them had published in years." When the chair came to the department, an associate professor—one who hadn't published in 12 years—told him, "he didn't intend to do any research, that he enjoyed teaching, and asked why he should waste his time on research." In response, the chair "didn't challenge his values" but simply showed his support:

> The simple act of acknowledging and letting him know that I appreciated the things that he was doing and, when he contributed, I made it a point to go to him and say, just casually, "I really appreciated the leadership you provided."

Follow Up on the Plan

A final step in improving a faculty member's research performance is to follow up on the plan and strategies to determine whether an individual's productivity improves. Annual conferences or weekly meetings can be used as valuable time to assess progress. In some cases, you might see only a modest improvement. One individual said, "We haven't gotten to the point that he's doing any research, but he's talking about it." Another chair commented on the case of a tenured assistant professor in a comprehensive college who lacked a record of scholarly performance. Expectations for this individual were not high:

> I felt it necessary to get him involved in writing, or at least presenting papers where he needed to conduct a literature search to find relevant studies in his field, and then, hopefully, organize some proposals or *a* proposal to develop a research or scholarly study.

When individuals produce, consider promoting or advocating the person's cause by writing positive recommendations for promotion and tenure and visiting with faculty and administrators about the successful performance of the individual.

Conclusion

This chapter has outlined the importance of scholarly work in departments and suggested a framework to encourage such development. Strategies for development of the departmental culture as well as strategies for individual development have been presented. Finally, a four-step process for addressing issues related to research productivity has been provided as a guide for chairs. We advise that you reflect on the unique characteristics of your department and its members and that you adapt the model presented in this chapter to your specific needs.

As you contemplate your overall strategy for improving the scholarship of faculty in your department, and as you devise appropriate intervention strategies to promote research productivity, you might wish to consider the following questions as prompts:

- What is your vision of scholarly activity for your department?
- What steps need to be taken to accomplish this vision?

- Who are the people in the department who can model the desired scholarly behavior?
- What support is there to move this effort forward?

Endnotes

1. Kübler-Ross (1975, p. 10) discusses the five stages of dying as denial, rage and anger, bargaining, depression, and acceptance.

2. We chose to use categories representing a modification of causes discussed by Mager and Pipe (1970, pp. 101–104). They suggest that individuals might ask themselves: Is it a skill deficiency? Is the desired performance punishing? Is nonperformance rewarding to the individual? Does performance really matter? Are there obstacles to performing?

Suggested Resources

Bland, C. J., Weber-Main, A. M., Lund, S. M., & Finstad, D. A. (2005). *The research-productive department: Strategies from departments that excel.* Bolton, MA: Anker.

This is a qualitative study of research-productive departments at a major public research university. Not only are these research quality departments examined in-depth, the authors review the literature of research productivity in each of the 13 aspects they have identified as critical. Overarching these specific strategies are three aspects: individual characteristics of researchers, institutional characteristics, and leadership characteristics of the organization.

Boyer, E. L. (1990). *Scholarship reconsidered: Priorities of the professoriate.* Princeton, NJ: The Carnegie Foundation for the Advancement of Teaching.

This is a classic work that broadened the discussion about what scholarship is. Boyer suggests that the classically emphasized and rewarded *discovery* is only one form of scholarship. Other forms include integration, application, and teaching. This framework for scholarship has been adopted in many institutions and departments. It often provides a useful starting point in discussing the nature of scholarship.

Creswell, J. W. (1985). *Faculty research performance: Lessons from the sciences and the social sciences* (ASHE/ERIC Higher Education Report No. 4). Washington, DC: Association for the Study of Higher Education.

Creswell synthesizes the literature on faculty research performance over a 40-year period, which provides a good background to today's research. He discusses the measures of performance, the correlates of high productivity, and the conceptual explanations of scholarship available in the sociological and social-psychology literature. Overall, Creswell cites networking opportunities and environmental, sociological, and institutional factors as primary causes influencing research productivity.

Curry, T. H. (2006, February). Faculty performance reviews. *Effective Practices for Academic Leaders*, *1*(2), 1–16.

The author provides a framework to consider performance reviews within the institutional context and emphases. He provides various examples of plans, feedback letters, and other articles to use performance reviews to reach institutional and individual goals. Scholarly performance is one aspect that is emphasized in this briefing with suggestions for addressing various concerns and problems. A list of useful, more extensive references is also included.

Mager, R. F., & Pipe, P. (1970). *Analyzing performance problems*. Belmont, CA: Fearon Pitman.

Mager and Pipe wrote this concise work for managers and trainers who attempt to assess and solve problems in worker productivity. The book takes less than an hour to read and is well worth the time spent. The writing is organized in an "if–then" problem analysis flowchart format. A discussion in each chapter follows the progression of the chart. The tendency to solve every problem is discussed and refuted. Skill deficiencies are considered on three levels: lack of knowledge, lack of practice, and lack of effective feedback. Performance management is discussed as a tool for motivating workers to complete tasks that they don't/won't do. The final chapter contains a chart and "Quick Reference Checklist" summary that could be used by those without time to read the whole book.

O'Meara, K., & Rice, R. E. (2005). *Faculty priorities reconsidered: Rewarding multiple forms of scholarship*. San Francisco, CA: Jossey-Bass.

This reference provides an in-depth look at the four forms of scholarship proposed by Boyer. The authors provide some historical perspective as well as examples of each of the four types. The book provides useful perspectives for department chairs with examples of development and implementation from the various Carnegie classified institutions.

Seldin, P. (1980). *Successful faculty evaluation programs*. New York, NY: Coventry Press.

This work traces several forces that contribute to an increased research emphasis on college campuses. Seldin examines faculty evaluation from several perspectives. Two chapters, "Institutional Service" and "Research and Publication," are of special interest.

Thomas, J. R. (2006, May). Fostering scholarly research in departments and colleges. *Effective Practices for Academic Leaders*, *1*(5), 1–16.

This briefing provides an overview of the chair's role in facilitating research in the department, activities to encourage scholarly individual and collective work, and strategies to support faculty research. The author provides suggestions for hiring, helping new faculty (including some thoughts on mentoring), and reinvigorating established faculty research. Several useful resources are provided.

Wergin, J. F. (2003). *Departments that work: Building and sustaining cultures of excellence in academic programs*. Bolton, MA: Anker.

Wergin has studied departments for many years in an attempt to find characteristics of excellence. The book addresses tough issues such as what is quality, motivation of faculty, evaluation criteria, criteria of an engaged department, and departmental values. He suggests several questions that departments should ask and provides examples of poor evaluation questions. The overall focus is on creating a culture of evidence about quality that is built from the inside out.

8

Refocus Faculty Efforts

*Higher education succeeds or fails in terms of motiva-
tion, not cognitive transfer of information.*
—Csikszentmihalyi, 1982

Some faculty members find new challenges and maintain enthusiasm throughout their careers. With gentle prodding and suggestions, others find renewed vigor. Some find it through expanding
or modifying their areas of interest, others through sabbaticals or
leaves of absence. Some faculty, however, need help initiating a
major refocus in their work to remain productive and excited about
their careers.

Refocusing might become necessary due to lack of motivation,
changing family dynamics, personality difficulties, aging issues, or
because of shifts in the priority or mission of an academic department. Faculty might have little control over a changing work environment that renders their skills or areas of expertise seemingly
obsolete for departmental needs and goals. Similarly, the associated
increased responsibilities that a senior faculty member encounters
with additional committee assignments or administrative duties can
serve as unavoidable distractions in the pursuit of continued academic productivity.

In our interviews, chairpersons spoke about their responsibility
for assisting faculty to refocus their efforts and clearly indicated that

chairs should be a force in helping faculty move ahead with their professional lives. They also emphasized that helping faculty is not simply a technical series of events that can be laid out and forgotten, but a process of negotiating and renegotiating efforts and rewards.

Determining the most appropriate reward for each faculty member is paramount in facilitating motivation. Success in faculty motivation is dependant on the depth of knowledge about the personal characteristics of each faculty member (Bess, 1982). Traditional incentives, such as increased responsibility, recognition, or money, might not be a motivational factor for every faculty member and especially not with senior tenured faculty. If we adapt the work of Buckingham and Coffman (1999) to higher education, it suggests that every faculty member does not have to be treated equally to achieve motivational success. Rather, an individualized reward or incentive structure must be developed for each person. While additional administrative activities are important early in a faculty member's career to promote professional vitality, these same diversions can impair and distract from continued growth over time.

A music chairperson with five years of experience noted that faculty productivity is a result of them being "happy." The chair should also recognize that rewards might be only a short-term incentive and might not translate into long-term faculty satisfaction unless the reward contributes to an overall improved departmental performance and, hence, an improved work environment. Another chair commented that "one of the most important and certainly one of the most satisfying things I have ever done as chair is to meet toward the end of every semester with every assistant professor to have a serious, frank discussion about scholarship, teaching, and service."

This concern with the range of needs and development stages is addressed by Bland and Risbey (2006):

> But in our fast changing world even the most accomplished faculty can become obsolete, lack the ability to

keep up with their institution's increasing use of technology or feel undervalued and disconnected from the mission, vision and ongoing work of the department. Consistent lack of development puts faculty at risk of becoming stagnant or "stuck" and losing motivation to complete their tasks. (p. 8)

This chapter explores the process that chairs might use to help faculty refocus their efforts. This process consists of four steps:

- Detect the signs of a developing concern through information gathering.
- When the issue is validated, explore options with the individual by assessing feelings, needs, and interests.
- Mutually design a plan for intervention that includes coming to an agreement on goals and proposed direction.
- Arrange for activities, resources, and feedback to implement the plan.

Detect the Signs of Lack of Focus

The forces leading to change are complex and often difficult to identify. However, an astute chair might observe early signs that faculty are not experiencing continued vigor. If faculty do not make the necessary adjustments, their behavior might become chronic and disruptive to the intradepartmental dynamics with other faculty, as well as to the faculty member's students and advisees. It might also lead to further disengagement on the part of the faculty, which perpetuates the cycle. Thus, it is important for chairpersons to gather information about potential motivational concerns through personal observations, annual evaluation conferences, and from visiting with students and colleagues. Although, admittedly, most faculty are intrinsically motivated, external evaluation through an informational, nonpunitive manner might be beneficial.

Chairs might look for signs that include:

- *Dissatisfaction with work roles or assignments:* A chairperson at a research university provided an example: "Many faculty were hired as specialists, and it seemed that every time somebody was hired, it took away from something he was doing. It reached a point where he obviously was just given whatever was left or needed to be picked up. There was very little professional opportunity left for this individual."

- *Lack or loss of enthusiasm, getting stale, or suffering burnout:* A chairperson at a liberal arts college talked about a person who "started to come to class late and withdrew into herself." A political science chair who has been engaged in academic work for more than 20 years noted that, "for a lot of faculty, the next 10 years should not be identical to the last 10 years."

- *Performing minimal duties, doing only what crosses their desks:* A chair at a comprehensive university talked about "a person [who] taught classes and that's about all he did."

- *Negative attitude:* A chair at a research university reported a case of a faculty member who "was perceived by others as not having a positive attitude. He responded negatively and defensively." Another chair encountered faculty who expressed a desire to decide on their own "what we want to do and then tell the rest of the department. We really don't want you as a chair or the rest of the department to weigh in on this."

- *Post-tenure review:* Several institutions now have a post-tenure review process that might surface professional and personal performance issues. Some are reviews for all faculty while others are triggered by

Table 8.1. Characteristics of movers and stuck faculty.

Characteristic	Movers	Stuck
Aspirations	High goals	Low goals; loss of enthusiasm
Self-esteem	Self-confident; willing to take risks	Low self-esteem; cautious/conservative; looks for formulas
Connection to work	A workaholic	Becomes disengaged; "retires on the job"; spends time off campus or on outside pursuits (e.g., professional associations)
Relationships	Keeps political alliances alive; concerned about larger issues in the organization	Falls back on protective peer groups; seeks outside sources for esteem
How dissatisfaction is handled	Active, constructive forms of protest; feels decision-makers will listen	Petty griper; subtle saboteur; blocks committee work; resists innovation; makes life difficult for others

Source: Kanter (1981, pp. 36–37)

poor performance (Licata & Morreale, 2006). Kanter
(1981) describes individuals who are "movers" and
those who are "stuck" in their jobs. Characteristics of
both types of individuals, shown in Table 8.1, might be
useful for department chairs who are looking for signs
of a problem.

Explore Options with the Individual

A chair revealed that one of the "challenges of the job is trying to support somebody when in your heart of hearts you think that they should do it another way." Another chair asserted that you cannot legislate productivity and, in effect, success is achieved when faculty are "given the freedom to be productive [and to] create as much as possible a climate where people can optimize their abilities," as this will provide the best results. If any of the signs previously described are present, consider exploring options with the individual by assessing feelings, interests, and needs. This step involves the crucial practices of listening, understanding, and comforting. For example, a business department chair finds that an effective means to identify a faculty member's strengths and motivations is through "informal door to door chatting, the walk about, the being there, being visible, being interested, taking time to listen."

Furniss (1981), an advocate of faculty career changes, speaks of the challenges associated with motivational issues:

> The motivational questions are tough ones for the established academic. They are probably toughest at the stage when the faculty member has not yet acknowledged the strength of the push to change what he is doing and has discussed it with no one. A common element to all the techniques of intervention in career counseling and personal therapy is providing the environment in which the client will begin to talk about [a] situation with a view to improving it and not just complaining about it. (p. 100)

Regarding a senior faculty member who faced changing institutional expectations for scholarly work, a chairperson at a doctoral-granting school said:

> He had my full support. I was empathetic and understanding about his inactivity in research performance because it was not being reinforced. I let him know I did

not expect immediate turnaround and that over a period of years we expected to see him get back into the mainstream.

Unfortunately, some faculty get mired in routines or ruts and cannot overcome the inertia by themselves. Unless someone—sometimes a colleague but more often the chair—initiates an active exploration process, a faculty member might begin a downward spiral that is difficult to reverse. He or she becomes isolated and disenchanted. When this happens, all parties lose—faculty member, chairperson, student, department, and the institution. If this situation can be changed, everyone can gain.

Effecting change and providing the opportunity for continued growth can be facilitated by creating an environment of imbalance between a faculty member's skills and challenges (Csikszentmihalyi, 1990). This imbalance must be measured so it does not create a circumstance that is counterproductive by generating angst and frustration on the part of the involved faculty. Success requires both motivation and skills. A chair at a comprehensive college responded with a sense of creative exploration when a senior faculty member expressed a desire to do something new:

> Several years ago a faculty member in his late 50s was getting stale. He wanted to have a new opportunity. He liked to travel and went abroad every summer. The department has numerous foreign students in whom the professor had always shown an interest. Their language skills were often poor. Perhaps he would like to gain the skills to teach them English as a second language? I noted a further benefit. When he retired he would have a skill that would let him get a job in all sorts of fascinating places. He is now getting a master's in teaching English as a second language.

In the process of exploration, the chair helped the faculty member blend individual strengths and interests with departmental needs.

While carving out a teaching area that the department wanted, the individual was also setting himself up with skills useful for retirement or a second career.

Successful exploration of options requires considerable reality testing. As one chairperson explained:

> I am getting them to think through the options. I say, "This is the direction the department is going, and it will be hard for you to get back into the mainstream. We can try for that, or we can try to get you into something else in the university."

If there is a level of trust and support, one can mention almost any option and the discussion will be seen as helpful, even if the option represents a major change, such as working in a different campus unit or seeking employment at another institution. To develop this point further, the same chairperson reported that his department had several nonresearchers who "moved on." "But," he emphasized, "that doesn't mean they were booted out." For example, one member, a clinician, is now working at the campus clinical center where "he is happy." The importance of finding the unique match of interests and needs was further clarified by another chair:

> People are different. If you try and blend them into a mold, they'll resist because they are not comfortable with it. But if you work with them to find their strengths and interests (all the people we're working with are intelligent), most of them can make contributions.

Helping a faculty member clarify feelings about his or her personal situation calls for one-on-one conversations between the chair and the individual with the application of active listening skills. A chair in business described a long-time department member who had experienced burnout:

> He taught classes and that was about all; he was perceived by others as not having a positive attitude, but

that was just the way in which he expressed himself. We have now made significant progress in turning the situation around.

In refocusing situations, when chairs and faculty explore feelings as well as professional and personal satisfactions, it leads to defining options or alternatives that might fit the interests of the faculty member. The discovery process often moves slowly, and it requires numerous conversations and a substantial time commitment. In some of the classical literature and in adult development research, this time of moving from the old (known) to the new (unknown) requires some "wandering through the wilderness" or experiencing what Bridges (1980) describes as the "neutral zone." At this critical stage in a person's career, the availability of a chairperson and colleagues who are prepared to listen can lessen the anguish and ease the transition.

Mutually Design a Plan for Intervention

When the faculty member commits to retrain in a new area or refocus his or her efforts, the chair can help the individual develop and structure a plan. A term from the social-psychology field, *psychological contract*, captures the essence of this step (Schein, 1978). The term is described in considerable detail by Rousseau (1995). Through various kinds of symbolic and actual events, a psychological contract is formed, which defines what the employee will give in terms of effort and contributions in exchange for challenging or rewarding work, acceptable working conditions, organizational rewards in the form of pay and benefits, and an organizational future in the form of a promise of promotion or other forms of career advancement. This contract is psychological in that the actual terms remain implicit: They are not written down anywhere. But the mutual expectations formed between the employee and the employer function like a contract in that if either party fails to meet the expectations, serious consequences will follow, including demotivation, turnover, lack of advancement, or termination (Schein, 1978).

Chairs should also be alert to what has been defined as the unilateral contract, which occurs when a faculty member believes that someone in the organization, often a former chair or dean, indicated that if the individual accomplished particular tasks or developed certain products, then he or she would be rewarded through promotion or some other kind of reward. A new chair is often not aware of the situation and wonders why the faculty member expresses disappointment or anger toward the chair or the institution. Situations of this nature require helping the faculty member get over the resentment and understand that a new contract can be established with the new chair.

Although faculty are loath to consider themselves "employees," and chairpersons are not traditionally viewed as "employers," the contract model is useful because it emphasizes the implicit or unwritten rules that can operate between chairs and their faculty. In view of changes during a faculty member's career, one element of this contract is continual negotiation between chairs and their faculty. Schein (1978) puts the case for needing to renegotiate the contract at different career stages:

> The psychological contract changes in important ways as the person goes through a career and life cycle, because his or her needs change in major and subtle ways. Similarly, what the organization expects of the individual changes with changes in conditions, job or role. Thus, one might expect that in the mid- and late-career there is a growing likelihood that new disappointments will arise because the individual effort and the organization's rewards may be based upon assumptions which were more appropriate to an earlier career or life stage. Rather than re-motivating the person, a better solution might be to renegotiate the psychological

contract and to adjust expectations on both sides to new realities. (p. 122)

In addition to the psychological commitment of the two parties, the contract can translate into acquisition of resources, reduction of bureaucratic obstacles, and reassignment of duties.

Arrange for Activities, Resources, and Feedback

Department chairs expressed various views about their roles in facilitating faculty development. One chair pictured himself as a facilitator: "I simply provide the platform on which everybody can participate." This role was identified as "useful in terms of strengthening my own relationship with colleagues in the department." Another department chair with 17 years of experience commented that the chair's role is to "serve as a cheerleader."

When an agreement has been reached with the faculty member on goals and a proposed direction, the chairperson should complete the four-step refocusing process: identify a sequence of activities, such as schedule changes; reduce or reassign teaching loads; or possibly even expand faculty teaching responsibilities in hopes of reenergizing the enthusiasm of their early academic career. In institutions that do not weigh teaching in promotional efforts, this option might only be viable for tenured faculty. As a seasoned chair, you might consider this to be an absurd option. While not a traditional or conventional approach, this suggestion is meant to serve as a reminder that there is no boilerplate approach; thinking outside the box to find an individualized solution utilizing traditional as well as nontraditional approaches might, on occasion, be required. A time frame would then need to be established to meet the goals, as one chair observed: "Commit resources and support for the activities, such as student or clerical help, travel to meetings and internship sites, educational materials, tuition payments, and professional leaves."

A chair of a political science department maintained that to motivate faculty to do things that they have not done before, "you need some carrots and sticks," even though there simply aren't many carrots and sticks available. The chair also noted that "trying to mold behavior and trying to push faculty into things they particularly don't want to do is the hardest part of your job."

Of course, the amount of resources available to chairs can vary greatly. One chair noted that "professional development activities related to faculty are very minimal because there's not that much money running down the pipe to attend conferences and seminars." Others noted that while a certain level of funding was available, it was often not sufficient and that faculty members frequently had to shoulder the burden of conference costs. At another extreme, some chairs commented on numerous workshops offered by their college and a very active faculty development department with annual meetings with each faculty member. One chair noted that "right now every day there are development opportunities for faculty here on campus. There isn't a day of the week that we don't have something for faculty or staff."

Conclusion

A chair's role is to creatively help faculty move in new directions and to identify resources for these moves. Without such efforts, unsatisfactory situations are often ignored, and no adjustments are made to develop the kind of relationship necessary for continued productivity. The preceding examples show the chairperson's ability to assess talent and be able to negotiate the psychological contract as a means of integrating departmental and individual needs.

Some institutions provide formal programs to help faculty develop refocusing plans. Here is one proposed structure of a faculty renewal and redirection program:

1. Situational statement:

   - Where are you now?
   - What needs to be modified or changed?

2. Goals and objectives:

   - What goals are you trying to achieve?
   - How will this benefit you?
   - How will this benefit the institution?

3. Activities and timetable to realize the goals and objectives:

   - What are the first steps?
   - What is the sequence of activities and expected time frame? (A flowchart or similar method might be helpful.)

4. Support needed to realize the plan:

   - What resource people are needed to accomplish the objectives?
   - What will they do?
   - What financial resources are needed? Where will you get them?
   - What support (including allocated time) do you need from administrators?

5. Evaluation of the plan:

   - How will you know when you achieve the objectives?
   - Who else can help you measure your accomplishments?
   - How will you monitor your progress en route?

6. Future directions after the plan:

   - What future steps will be important?

Although the questions might be different in other growth programs, the identified common elements are the opportunities for career assessment, development of peer and administrative support, and the identification of new growth experiences.

If you have identified a need to assist one or more of your faculty to refocus their efforts, you might wish to begin thinking about responses to the following questions:

- What are the priorities of the department?
- How can established faculty be redirected to meet these needs?
- What new psychological contracts should be renegotiated?
- What resources are available or can be found to help this redirection?
- What structures are needed for individuals to be successful?

Suggested Resources

Bland, C. J., & Bergquist, W. H. (1997). *The vitality of senior faculty members: Snow on the roof—fire in the furnace* (ASHE-ERIC Higher Education Report, Vol. 25, No. 7). Washington, DC: The George Washington University, Graduate School of Education and Human Development.

   This resource focuses particularly on mid-career and late-career faculty. It provides information on motivation and interests of faculty who are too often written off by the institution. Of particular interest are the findings that senior faculty have similarities to other faculty and can derive similar benefits to those gained by other faculty.

Bland, C. J., & Risbey, K. R. (2006, July). Faculty development programs. *Effective Practices for Academic Leaders, 1*(7), 1–16.

   Although the primary focus is on institution-wide faculty development efforts, this resource provides several useful strategies and resources to address faculty at various career stages. Of particular interest is the tie between institutional vitality and faculty development. The suggestion is that established faculty can redirect to address important institutional needs.

Bridges, W. (1980). *Transitions: Making sense of life's changes*. Reading, MA: Addison-Wesley.

Still one of the best resources on personal transitions, Bridges describes the personal change process involved in moving from one life situation or position to another. He describes a "neutral zone" between endings and beginnings. Someone in a neutral zone needs a guide to progress through the transition. Words or actions might be less important or helpful than the fact that someone is available.

Furniss, W. T. (1981). *Reshaping faculty careers*. Washington, DC: American Council on Education.

Furniss was one of the first authors to explicitly address creative options in faculty career development. He provides a range of possibilities within and outside the academy for mid- and late-career academics to satisfy their career needs. Given today's financial constraints and pressures, chairs have to work even harder at finding alternatives, particularly outside the department.

Rousseau, D. M. (1995). *Psychological contracts in organizations: Understanding written and unwritten agreements*. Thousand Oaks, CA: Sage.

The author examines the organizational, social, and psychological meaning of all kinds of written and unwritten contracts. With the tremendous changes in contracting due to changes in the environment, this reference is rich in ideas and examples.

Schein, E. (1978). *Career dynamics: Matching individual and organizational needs*. Reading, MA: Addison-Wesley.

Schein provides a useful and pioneering work on examining careers in organizations. He offers suggestions for how insightful leaders and managers can satisfy individual and organizational needs. He highlights mid-career issues that particularly affect the psychological contract.

9

Address Personal Issues of Faculty

Chairpersons need to carefully assess their personal
reaction to the pain level of confronting personal
problems and initiate institutional procedures to help
faculty members.
　　　—A chair of philosophy at a major research university

It [addressing personal problems] was where I felt
most out of my element.
　　　—A chair of modern languages at a research university

The personal issues and problems of individual faculty members are a potential threat to the professional productivity of academic departments. Because institutions today often break the traditional psychological contracts (the quid pro quo agreements) and because we inhabit a more litigious environment, with concerns about being sued over a wide range of student, staff, and faculty issues, differentiating between personal and nonpersonal issues can be a major challenge. If individual problems are not addressed, others in the department will have to pick up the responsibility. Though chairs might feel out of their element and experience the pain of a frustrating and difficult situation, they are often called on by faculty and administrators to address the personal issues of faculty. Chairs should keep in mind that other resource people can play an important role in resolving or at least managing the issue.

The most commonly occurring personal situations can be categorized as follows:

- Relationship problems with students, staff, and faculty
- Difficulties associated with dual careers
- Exclusion and alienation in the department
- Health problems
- Personal disorganization
- Relationship between family and employment
- Institutional affiliation and commitment

In response to these issues, how can chairpersons assist faculty with personal difficulties? Reflect on the following questions as you read this chapter:

- Is the personal issue of the faculty member short term or long term (chronic)?
- What are the signs of an individual with a short-term problem?
- What strategies can a chair use with a short-term problem?
- What are the signs of an individual with chronic personal problems?
- What strategies can a chair use with a long-term (chronic) problem?
- What strategies can a chair use to address faculty career and family work?

Differentiate Between Short- and Long-Term Issues

Short-term issues are those of limited duration that diminish in importance or disappear quickly. Personal crises such as individual loss, change in family or financial status, and medical issues can create situations in which faculty members temporarily demonstrate a lack of concentration, emotional distress, and disorientation. From the adult development literature, we know these crises and demands are predictable life experiences and that, with emotional support and some direct help, individuals usually work their way through them and make adjustments. In these types of situations, people are just trying to achieve balance in their lives.

Chairs might look for the following signs of problems:

- *Severe loss or separation:* death of a significant other or divorce
- *Changes in family status:* children leaving; children coming back home; aging parents; elderly parents moving into the house; single-parent status
- *Changes in work status:* having a new job or role; adjusting to a mate having a job outside the home or new job; staying employed beyond the former traditional age; retirement
- *Added financial responsibility:* buying a house; sending children to college
- *Personal aging issues:* physical changes; passing age benchmarks (e.g., 40, 50, 60); loss of energy; transition issues with the institution
- *Health problems:* anxiety about health; short-term surgery; short-term depression
- *Student issues:* cheating and plagiarism

Adopt Strategies for Temporary Problems

We recommend several strategies for addressing temporary personal problems:

- *Become aware of the concern* through heart-to-heart talks and listening to the individual.
- *Protect the individual* during the troubled time by being a buffer for a short period, reducing demands or workload, and adjusting responsibilities so the individual can take time off to address his or her needs.

- *Seek outside help* by referring the individual to counselors for short-term psychological help or enlisting the
  help of senior faculty who know the individual.

Sometimes personal problems persist and become chronic.
Working with long-term problems can be frustrating. These problems include alcoholism, psychiatric disorders, habitual interpersonal difficulties, inability to cope with departmental and academic
expectations, and individual personality traits such as difficult and
uncooperative behaviors, aggressive behaviors, "weird behaviors"
(e.g., blurting out, off-color comments), and severe withdrawal.

The following brief scenarios illustrate situations that chairpersons might encounter:

- A philosophy chair at a major research university discussed the case of a 50-year-old full professor who frequently cancelled classes and reported being sick. The
  graduate students began to draw away from him. The
  quality and quantity of his work was on a downhill
  slide. Junior faculty were covering more and more of
  his responsibilities, yet he was in the regular salary
  range with everyone else as if nothing was happening.
  This caused a morale problem within the department.
- A chair of a music department in a comprehensive university described a faculty member who was past 65 but
  wouldn't have to retire until he was 70. He had serious
  health problems, which left him with little energy,
  although he was a well-respected faculty member.
- A plant sciences chair at a land-grant university
  described a faculty member who had been difficult and
  uncooperative. "I found a negative attitude toward him
  by faculty in the department, especially senior faculty."
- A chair of a criminal justice department at a comprehensive university told of "an outspoken, critical,
  impetuous, short-fused faculty member. My first day on

the job I went to her lab where she proceeded to rant and rave for 30 minutes about her disappointment with professional opportunities, with her colleagues, and with the progress of the department."

- A chair of a music department at a comprehensive university commented about an outstanding academic who, by the third year, was "completely bogged down" in coursework and "became very paranoid. He thought the students were doing things to him, didn't sleep for weeks on end, and blurted out bizarre things. It was obvious he needed psychiatric help."

- A chair of an English department at a comprehensive university described a faculty member with severe family problems. "It involves his wife, who has mental problems. It's just a very difficult situation in terms of her willingness to be helped. She thinks that everybody else has the problem. She's been hospitalized and institutionalized a couple times."

These long-term issues require more elaborate interventions than the short-term issues.

Adopt Strategies for Intervening in Chronic Cases

A chairperson in criminal justice at a comprehensive college talked about a general process model he would use with faculty experiencing chronic problems. Four steps were involved: developing an awareness of the issue; holding a "colleague-to-colleague" discussion about the issue; using the authority of the chair position; and, if necessary, initiating formal procedures to modify faculty behavior.

Develop an Awareness of the Issue

As with all professional–personal development issues and concerns, chairs need to be aware of signs and symptoms. These include gathering information through personal observations (e.g., looking for withdrawal, aggressiveness, and mental difficulties) and obtaining feedback from students and colleagues. Without this fundamental awareness, the helping process will be ungrounded. In this step, the practices of observing, listening, and probing are particularly crucial.

Hold a Colleague-to-Colleague Discussion

"Chairpersons initiate the first level of response as a colleague and friend," one chair said. The message you want to convey is, "I have a concern and how can I help you?" There is encouragement to get whatever help is needed to address the issue. This colleague-to-colleague attention was summarized by an associate of one chair who said, "He talks to people for a living." Other chairs in our study also reinforced the colleague-to-colleague discussion approach.

A chair of a drama department at a liberal arts college suggested initiating these conversations: "It's something I do because I cherish my colleagues. It's something I would be doing whether I was a chairperson or not." This colleague-to-colleague involvement was emphasized by a chair of history at a comprehensive university: "I get involved in their lives—not merely academics but financial matters and problems with children."

Chairs realize that it's not always easy to have these conversations, but they sometimes achieve results because the faculty realize there is a problem and that modifications at this stage might avoid more formal and adversarial procedures later. Establishing an open atmosphere and giving feedback are particularly useful, as indicated in the following suggestions provided by chairs:

- Allow the person to vent initially.
- Listen to the reason that deadlines are missed, and let her express her ideas.
- Do not minimize the problem, instead confront him with the problem.
- Stress the importance of meeting deadlines and how it affects others.
- Create a professional crisis equal to the personal crisis.

The challenge of assisting faculty in balancing their careers and family work is one most department chairs have to face as they recruit, hire, and retain faculty. Many institutions have formal policies in place that address issues such as tenure clock stop; modified duties leave; paid and unpaid dependent care leave; reduced, part-time, and job share assignments; paid leave following childbirth; and employment assistance for spouses or partners of faculty. Chairs need to utilize these policies and procedures and be as flexible as possible in addressing the balance of work and family. Curtis (2005), an advocate of balancing faculty career and work, indicated: "Perhaps the most daunting new challenge is that of stimulating a cultural change in the academy, so that faculty members who want to make use of policies for balancing work and family feel confident in doing so" (p. 2).

Use the Authority of Your Position

If you are unsuccessful in modifying behavior by persuading a colleague to seek help, use a more direct intervention to address the issue. You might wish to consider the following options that are supported by observations from experienced chairs:

- *Providing new areas of responsibility for the individual:* "I removed him from an assignment he felt inadequate about and reassigned him to other duties."
- *Having the individual see how others addressed problems:* "I had faculty eat breakfast together once a month away from the university, or I got him involved in workshops to give him insight into other people's problems."
- *Referring the individual to counselors or self-help groups:* "I encouraged him to go into counseling, or I assisted in getting him psychiatric help."

The chairs noted that this phase requires patience, skill, and innovation, and it provides clear messages to the individual: I'm here to see you get help; I'll take you out of class or whatever is necessary, but continuing the same pattern is unacceptable. Faculty members in this circumstance have crossed over the line of being responsible for their own behavior, and the chair must intervene.

Quite often chair intervention leads to outside referrals for counseling or psychiatric help. The use of an outside referral system is illustrated by a chair of a natural sciences department at a land-grant research university who described a highly emotional faculty member in the following manner:

> The faculty member is a hard-driving person who doesn't let up. These pressures mounted and resulted in a couple of emotional blowups with yelling and door slamming in the office of an administrator. A personal friend who knows his family suggested a history of manic-depressive behavior. I've pointed out to him examples of my behavior to prove I considered him trustworthy and to prove I dealt honestly and openly with him. I've had a number of very patient discussions with him. I made an extra effort to follow through on any commitments to him. Some of the administration think he's still a bomb waiting to go off. We have managed to get him psychological counseling. He may need psychiatric help.

As this example demonstrates, chairpersons are forced to make mental health assessments, however tentative, and to aid individuals in entering the mental health system for treatment.

A chair of a philosophy department at a major research university took the approach of referring the individual for outside help and lessening workload demands:

> This was an individual who came to us as a Ph.D. candidate. He was finishing his degree at a Big Ten School, had strong professional experience, and very good academic credentials. We had expected a great deal out of him. As things turned out, he got bogged down in coursework, and I'm not sure of all the pressures. The

next thing we knew he was acting very funny—talking of not being able to sleep for weeks on end and just blurting things out.

It was very stressful for all of us. I set about getting him psychiatric help. I talked to him, tried to understand his problems, and worked through the [university] machinery so the man was able to get the help he needed with the full support of the school. I was able to wind my way through the bureaucracy and sort of grease the way so that things happened.

After a time, I gave him a semester off. Then I brought him back in the summer to let him try one course. That didn't work out satisfactorily, so I sent him home to rest again until fall. We gave him a course in the fall and he wasn't able to handle that. Finally, we just arranged for him to have full pay for the rest of the year and to make sure he was still on full-time status so he was able to get the kind of psychiatric help he needed.

Eventually, the faculty member left, but the chair believed that the strategies were successful in that he provided a "bridge" or "link" for the individual to leave after seeking several opportunities for him to step back into the academic setting. "Sometimes success is helping someone accept that the situation isn't going to work," concluded the chairperson.

College and university campuses often have assistance programs for individuals with personal issues. Employee or faculty assistance programs (often referred to as EAPs or FAPs) help faculty and staff confront problems that can seriously affect their productivity. Such programs provide initial counseling and referral for commonly occurring personal issues: marital and family problems, drug and alcohol abuse, personal financial issues, and emotional stress. Major trends identified by Derr (2005) are EAPs with a greater proportion of their work in individual consultation with administrators on how to handle personal problems with employees; integration of work–life and traditional EAP work; and more use of technology, including web sites, chat rooms, distance tools, and use of off-campus facilities. Key questions that chairs should ask themselves about the personal assistance network on their campus include:

- What resources are available to help a person with a chronic problem? Is there an off-campus EAP? Often the best sources of this information are other chairs, the human resources department, or the psychology department.
- If there is an EAP, who is eligible to use it? What services are offered? How are the services used? Who is the contact person?
- If there is not an EAP available, what other referrals are possible? Is there a medical center or campus clinic that will address personal issues?
- If institutionally sponsored services are not available, who would be available outside the institution, and what are the defined procedures for using the services?

Chairs need to personally know a resource they can contact for referrals or have someone they can call who will identify a creditable, effective mental health professional. These individuals might be a contact on or off campus. You need to have the sequence of procedures and actual people in mind *before* situations arise. Pre-planning will help to prevent impulse or panic decisions.

As a Last Resort, Initiate Formal Procedures

In some of the more inimical cases, formal procedures are needed to bring about changed behavior. These include:

- Formal certified letter of the concerns and reasons for the initiated procedure, which can include freezing salary or commencing some personnel action.

- A formal meeting with the individual to discuss the contents of the letter because, as one chair remarked, "they need to know the rules and expectations."
- Follow through on procedures initiated.

No doubt chairs prefer issues to be resolved with early action steps. When more formalized personnel procedures are employed, issues can become polarized with gut-wrenching consequences for all involved. For example, faculty in the department might choose sides or rush to the defense of the "persecuted" faculty member. In one case, the chairperson responded to faculty concerns about an individual by "achieving a departmental agreement on how to address the faculty member in crisis so that there would be no move to scapegoat him." Not surprisingly, chairs also monitor procedures and strategies to avoid violating due process that can trigger possible grievances or lawsuits. In this step, chairs need to demonstrate firmness as well as compassion. A good description of the ideal approach is succinctly stated by Fisher and Ury (1981) where they advise, "be soft on the people, hard on the problem" (p. 13).

Certainly, chairs' fears and anxieties sometimes inhibit formal actions. A social sciences chairperson at a comprehensive university captures the dilemma:

> There is more freedom and flexibility at the chair level, yet it is generally perceived [as] just the opposite. Rather than back into the formalized procedures, I begin to notify faculty when formal procedures are begun and, in many cases, suggest they may want to retain the services of an attorney, especially in sexual harassment or any suspected criminal cases.

As standard operating procedure, chairs need to keep upper-level administrators informed about what is happening and consult legal counsel on how to proceed within the expected institutional guidelines. They also should coach and enlist the help of other faculty in what they can do to help the individual and protect the integrity of the institution. On a more personal level, chairs might determine how they will respond when and if their own popularity, respect, and fairness come into question because of the pressure they put on faculty to make adjustments.

Consider whether there would be risk in *not* initiating procedures. Will the problem be passed on to the next chair? Will faculty hide behind a distorted concept of academic freedom that says, "I can do whatever I want—I'm not accountable?" If the choice is made not to address chronic personal problems, chairs should recognize that they are possibly compounding the situation for the individual faculty and for the department in the long run. Often individuals enter a downward spiral they cannot seem to reverse without help, and in the process they create morale problems for the department. Chair intervention can be uncomfortable in the short term. Confrontations can generate denial and acrimonious feelings, and the outcomes are unpredictable. In the long term, however, the intervention might create a break in destructive patterns and provide opportunities for new decisions by faculty.

Conclusion

As you face the challenges of dealing with both short-term and chronic personal issues of faculty, you might wish to consider the following questions:

- Does the department have procedures, both formal and informal, in place to address personal issues?
- What options are available if these should become long-term issues?
- What institutional resources are available to help with personal issues?

Chairs should keep in mind that personal issues can happen to anyone. Many are short term and require additional support and relief from some assignments. More chronic problems require concentrated, ongoing effort and firmness.

Suggested Resources

Boice, R. (1982). Counseling colleagues. *Personnel and Guidance Journal*, 61(4), 239–241.

> Robert Boice, a psychologist–faculty development specialist, has written about counseling colleagues and identification of personal issues. Boice sees difficulty in addressing personal issues because professionals feel "self-reliant" and are reluctant to seek help. He suggests that as professional pressures and changes multiply, more attention to personal concerns will be needed. Boice initially helped faculty with mental blocks in writing and soon was involved in helping faculty deal with personal issues.

Derr, W. D. (2005, March/April). Envisioning EAP's future by reflecting on its past. *Behavioral Health Management*, 25(2), 13–18.

> This article looks at the future of EAPs by examining the changes and expectations for the future. The basic premise is that "the already broad brush of EAPs has become very broad." The author examines demographic, technological, and economic trends. An interesting prediction is that "EAP professionals will be a limited group of professionals more aligned with the organizational development field rather than the clinical and behavioral sciences."

Leslie, D. W. (2006). *Faculty careers and flexible employment*. Retrieved November 1, 2007, from www.tiaacrefinstitute.org/research/policy/pol010106.html

> This research documents the increase of female faculty over the last five years and provides updated information on the faculty labor market with implications for personal issues such as campus child care, spousal employment, and flexible retirement policies. In particular, with new employees expecting greater flexibility and more personal and professional integration in their lives, this information becomes even more important.

Scanlon, W. F. (1986). *Alcoholism and drug abuse in the workplace: Employee assistance programs*. New York, NY: Praeger.

> Scanlon's book contains a review of employee assistance programs. It covers the history, philosophy, and functions of EAPs. The impact of alcohol and drug abuse on the United States is considered from historical, economic, corporate, and rehabilitation perspectives.

Schein, E. (1978). *Career dynamics: Matching individual and organizational needs.* Reading, MA: Addison-Wesley.

Part I of Schein's book, "The Individual and the Life Cycle," provides insight into and a conceptual framework for looking at personal development. Schein integrates ideas of numerous developmental theorists into a framework of useful observations about personal and family demands and expectations. He also suggests constructive coping strategies that are useful for department chairs.

Stein, S. A. (2002, September/October). Why work/life and EAP should be integrated. *Behavioral Health Management, 22*(5), 33–41.

This article makes the case that EAPs should address both substance abuse and life–work issues rather than separate these issues as is commonly done, particularly in large organizations. Reasons provided for this integration include one person to contact; many if not most of the issues are interrelated; and financial efficiency. Return on investment figures are determined to be quite positive.

TIAA-CREF Research Dialogue. (1988). *Employee assistance programs in educational institutions* (No. 16). New York, NY: TIAA-CREF Institute.

This dialogue allows chairpersons to view the nature and use of employee assistance. For a detailed account of the development and scope of EAPs in higher education also consult: Thoreson, R. W., & Hosokawa, E. P. (1984). *Employee assistance programs in higher education: Alcohol, mental health and professional development programming for faculty and staff.* Springfield, IL: Charles C. Thomas.

10

Employ Technology Wisely

[Technology] is all-encompassing across the board. I think every instructor, faculty member, and chair has to have a certain level of computer literacy. [It's] absolutely expected! The students are coming in with incredibly sophisticated knowledge and expect certain things from their faculty.

—A chair of a business department

In his keynote speech at the 24th Annual Academic Chairpersons Conference, William Tierney, director of the Center for Higher Education Policy Analysis at the University of Southern California, identified technology as one of five conditions of change in the 21st century that will affect higher education and, by extension, will become a factor shaping the environments in which department chairs work. Tierney suggested that the changing nature and expectations of the students of tomorrow will produce profound changes in how we interact in the classroom and in the ways that we think and learn, changes that are nothing short of revolutionary.

This chapter explores this disruptive nature of technology and documents several features of technology that affect the role of the department chair. As you read this chapter we suggest that you keep these questions in mind:

- How has technology affected your discipline, your programs, teaching, and research within your department?
- What technology skills will your students need when they graduate, and what are the expectations of their future employers?
- How has your program curriculum and pedagogy changed, and does it use technology in appropriate ways and at appropriate levels?
- Is technology being used effectively to engage students in the learning experience and to foster active learning?
- Does your program have sufficient technology-related resources, and what strategies are in place to add or maintain necessary technology tools?

Be Aware of Technological Developments

It is hard to find a publication relating to higher education that does not contain articles or references to the use and application of technology in learning, research, and support services. The U.S. Department of Education (2004) highlighted the need to make technology an integral component of instruction in K–12, and there is an increasing call more generally for the integration of technology into teaching and learning at all levels. Organizations and projects such as the Teaching, Learning, and Technology Group (Gilbert); the Flashlight Project (Ehrmann); MERLOT (California State University); the Western Cooperative for Educational Telecommunications (WCET); the Roadmap to Redesign; the Sloan Foundation, and the National Center for Academic Transformation (Twigg) provide a strong focus on the effective use and transformational nature of technology in education.[1]

Few would argue that today's students and entering faculty engage in education in a much different environment than those who have participated in higher education for the past 20 or 30 years. Most higher education professionals readily acknowledge that today's students are quite different from students of 20 or even 10 years ago. They differ in their expectations of the college environment and in their expectations of the learning experience itself. They come from a world where technology is an integral part of their lives and often is simply taken for granted, and they expect technology to serve them not only in their social and recreational pursuits but also as a medium that provides unrestricted access to educational services and knowledge. They are more likely to define their educational activities in terms of collaboration and sharing. They view technology-based interaction (IMing, iPods, cell phones, and text messaging) as a way of life and as an adjunct to face-to-face encounters. They expect information on demand at their fingertips, and they view themselves as both consumers and creators of information.

Students entering college in the 21st century cannot remember a time when computers and CDs did not exist; they have always had portable phones, cable, VCRs, microwaves, remote controls, and Walkmans. For them MTV has always been on television. The social, leisure, and work world of today is fully integrated with a pervasive use of technology and has created an environment where computers are taken for granted. Technology touches nearly every aspect of our lives, and higher education is no different.

Moreover, today's environment is more technologically complex than at any time in the history of civilization. Technology supports our communication, manages our money and environment, and brings the world into our living rooms and classrooms. The acceptance of technology has grown and expanded into a reliance on technology for parents, current and prospective students, current and prospective faculty members, alumni, businesses, governments, and administrators, all of whom expect pervasive real-time access to information.

As with the remainder of our environment, technology has become an integral part of a university campus. It is highly unlikely that a college or university can be competitive without a reliable and robust technology infrastructure. Given the pervasive nature of technology, it is not surprising that departmental units are being affected by technology and that technology, in its many forms, has become a significant issue for department chairs.

The extent and reach of technology in higher education means that today's department chairs must develop a reasonable level of knowledge and comfort regarding the use of technology by their faculty, staff, and students because chairs are increasingly expected to address their technology needs and issues. In addition, they must make decisions relating to such issues as the selection and allocation of resources, cost, effectiveness, and time management.

Department chairs are likely to find that technology is no longer a luxury in higher education but, rather, that it has become a necessity. As such, technology will be an unavoidable and integral part of the chair's roles and responsibilities. In the words of a business department chair with nine years of experience:

> It's huge! It's affecting teaching. It's affecting management. It's affecting the systems we have in the college for student registration. It's all-encompassing across the board. I think every instructor, faculty member, and chair has to have a certain level of computer literacy. Absolutely expected! The students are coming in with incredibly sophisticated knowledge and expect certain things from their faculty. So yes, it has had a big impact.

While the use of technology is seen throughout the fabric of university life, probably nowhere is the impact so profoundly felt as in the area of instruction. Not only has the integration of technology into the teaching and learning process expanded dramatically during the past decade, the technology supporting that integration has continued to change and advance and has brought with it an ever-increasing set of challenges. The chair of a biology department at a private college describes this changing landscape in the following way:

> In the last half dozen years or so, technology has just about permeated every level of our curricula here, particularly in the sciences. We have computer hookups and Internet hookups in all of our classrooms. We have many classrooms with built-in data projectors. One of the things that is happening with faculty now is a trend to move from desktop computers to laptops so they can just have their machines and plug them into the room that they're in. So, it's everywhere now. And that's happened quite rapidly.

The expanding and changing use of technology presents an entirely new set of issues for the department chair, which were, for the most part, nothing more than an occasional question a decade ago. Today, chairs must be aware of, become familiar with, and learn to address a wide range of technology issues. This is particularly true of issues that have a heavy technology overlay or component, such as those relating to faculty and staff technology literacy, communication efficiency, informed decision making, outcomes, assessment and accountability, budget and resource allocation, emergent use of courseware, and student services.

Encourage Faculty and Staff Technology Literacy

Technology has sparked a growing expectation among staff, faculty, and students. Though current skill levels in departments vary widely, the growing reliance on technology for departmental communication, instruction, and administration requires a working level of technology skill. Many chairs noted the issue of technology literacy expectations. A chair with 20 years of experience who leads an education department stated:

There's just an expectation for more and more technology. Just as an example, for accreditation visits we're expected to have electronic exhibits. What used to be called an exhibit room is now just simply a series of web sites where all of the material that used to be physical paper copies is now on the web site. Being familiar with that process, being able to work in that sort of environment affects how well you do your job.

Technology literacy among faculty has become an increasingly important issue. Department chairs find it necessary to deal with technology implications in terms of faculty expectation and faculty performance as well as in the hiring and promotion processes. In most educational settings, it is simply expected that faculty will use computers, as illustrated by the examples of faculty who can be assigned to teach online courses, must submit grades online, and increasingly are required to maintain an electronic portfolio for tenure and promotion and accreditation. Department chairs are often faced with a complex set of issues, including some faculty who expect to have robust and reliable technology immediately available; other faculty members who struggle with even the most basic technology tasks; and students who increasingly come to the educational environment more technically skilled than their instructors. A growing number of faculty—particularly those now entering the academy—expect that technology will automatically be available to them, often at levels beyond the reach of the current resources of the department or college. At the same time, the chair often finds it necessary to support other faculty who do not possess the necessary skills to deal with even the most basic of technology tools. One department chair in a Midwest public university recounted:

I guess some faculty barely know how to turn on the computer while others are developing fully online media-rich courses. We are adding the equipment to teach with technology at a relatively rapid rate now in terms of having projection devices in classes and laptops available to use for PowerPoint presentations and things like that. But that too is just sort of an emerging field where now there's expectation to do more with online assignments as a component of the course. Faculty use PowerPoint presentations quite commonly. Students in many cases are actually better at it than some of our faculty.

Support Technology Training

Because of the changing expectations for faculty and staff to be technology literate, gaps can form between older and newer faculty and staff and can present significant issues within a department, which can affect a department's ability to communicate and work effectively. Department chairs are recognizing the increased importance of having technology training, assistance, support, and professional development available to both faculty and staff. Chairs address this issue in a variety of ways. At one school the faculty professional development courses have been converted to online offerings so the faculty and staff can take them over the Internet at their own pace and in their own time. Other departments report conducting specific training courses or providing specific professional development opportunities for staff and faculty on different software packages and instructional technology resources. And yet other institutions have adopted approaches such as assigning technical advisors to various departments for resource training and support. A chair of a department of anthropology at a large research university told us: "We have things for secretarial staff, for example. There are various programs from how to use a particular package of software to how to deal with a difficult boss." And similar thoughts were expressed by a department chair at a small private college:

> We're in pretty good shape. And because of the resources that are available and because we have a very, very good

IT staff and a lot of support, it makes it easy for faculty with any interest at all to get to the technology and to learn how to use it. . . . We have computer and Internet hookups in all of our classrooms.

Use Technology Efficiently

As previously noted, faculty and staff are increasingly expected to possess a minimum level of technological literacy to perform basic functions such as communication, attendance reporting, grading, and so on. Communication is one of the areas most affected by the shift to a technology-dominant environment, which is clearly evident in the interaction between department members and between the students and faculty. Technology has manifestly changed the dynamics of most department communication through the use of email, blogs, podcasts, wikis, and other similar tools. And there is general acceptance that administrative technologies have provided hundreds of time-saving and time-effective advantages for departments and faculty.

Many chairs argue that the largest and probably most important impact of technology on the internal workings of the department and the chair is the speed with which information is transmitted and received. This ease and immediacy of communication was highlighted by many chairs we spoke to, including three chairs at different public universities, all of whom had considerable experience:

I would say that the major effect on the department chair has been the speed with which information can be retrieved and the speed with which information can be transmitted.

Email is the greatest thing that has ever happened to a chair because now, for every little thing, you don't have to call people on the phone or go visit them in their office.

I think that there's a lot more access to administrators now because of voice mail and email.

Technology has also impacted the academic unit by creating more efficient ways to organize office functions and to respond to the informational needs of faculty and students. Many department chairs we spoke to reported increased office effectiveness and efficiency because of technological advances. One chair at a Canadian university highlighted this issue:

> I think technology . . . has streamlined things. We're able to be better prepared to ask and answer a variety of questions coming from students, address curriculum issues. Things are recorded, we have archives of stuff, we don't have to flip through hard copies of a million books behind the course outline from 1988, we can pull it up on the computer. So, with those kinds of things, accessibility is better.

Similar thoughts were also expressed by a department chair at a two-year public institution: "We have a site where all the forms, all the rules and regulations the faculty have to follow, are set up there so that at a click from their office they can find the relevant information."

While technology has delivered much needed efficiency improvements in terms of communication and student support, it has also created some challenges. On one level, technology (specifically communications via email) has made the department chair much more accessible, placing a greater demand on the chair in terms of time. A chair of social work and a chair at a community college described this accessibility and demand in the following ways:

> Technology has really helped me make my job a bit easier but it has also placed more demands on me. I'm more accessible and so it's helped me in terms of communi-

cating with my faculty and students and administration, but on the other hand, it's made me more available.

Although technology offers some opportunities, it also offers a lot of challenges in terms of keeping things current and making sure that, again, access is something that's being considered.

Just as the speed and ease of technology-based communication can improve and increase interaction, it can also have unintended or undesirable consequences. Department chairs have become increasingly aware of the problems that can occur as a result of miscommunication within the department arising from the ease and immediacy of technology-based communications and the special care they must take to avoid them. A chair of English at a large public university described the problems of miscommunication in this way:

It's also meant that sometimes in terms of this climate issue that I've mentioned, people can respond impulsively and send some sort of impudent, ill-considered sort of angry email to somebody and then that person can forward it to the whole list and so on and so on. There's a way in which it's caused problems too.

Similar comments were provided by a chair of respiratory care at a community college:

But in doing so, it gets kind of cumbersome in terms of making sure that everybody's keeping up on that and has read the latest email and understands the changes of the previous one. So I think it's created some communication challenges, too, because it is so easy to just kind of flip out a little message and sometimes you have to be really, really careful that you are conveying what you want to convey, put the right tone to it, have the right information in it, and that you've had the needed discussion.

Use Technology to Facilitate Outcomes, Assessment, and Accountability

The importance of technology in the assessment process is one that chairs will be unable to avoid as calls for assessment and accountability increase and, arguably, become easier. Technology-based assessment and the attendant ease of collection, aggregation, and reporting of information have had significant effects on departmental procedures, expectations, and requirements. The increase in technology use has created a new level of evaluation for courses, faculty, and staff, as well as students. The ease of use and dissemination of technology-based assessment data have also increased accountability for departments and faculty and have increased their need to demonstrate quality in terms of instructional outcomes. As the amount and granularity of information about the results of a program or course are made available, faculty and departments will continue to find themselves under increasing pressure to address areas of weakness or to provide increased support to students. A chair of a sciences department at a regional university described the use and importance of outcomes assessment and accountability in this way:

> It seems that we've been changing those systems for curricular support in the instruction of students twice, three times in the last four or five years and that requires all of our faculty to learn a new system. So outcomes are important and we're trying to develop a system for assessing student outcomes at the course level, and then bring it up to, okay, what do you expect a freshman when they finish their first year to have in terms of outcomes.

The importance of performance indicators and accountability was echoed by a dean and former chair at a Canadian institution:

> I mean we have certain key performance indicators and our program report card that comes out every year with

all the statistics about if it's a clear program, and what's the percentage of students getting employed. And as dean now, I can see those report cards and try to have those early conversations with the chairs about steps that can be taken and action plans to be put into place.

The same technology that is being used to support the quality improvement initiatives of departments internally is readily available to respond to many of the external demands for accountability that come from accreditation agencies, governmental entities, and the public. In many cases, accreditation agencies are now requiring electronic artifacts of student performance through the use of e-portfolios to validate program integrity and to demonstrate student outcomes and competencies. A music department chair at a private college highlighted this use of technology:

> So that whole process really helps with our credibility to know that we are held in line with national standards that every other music institution, degree seeking or degree granting department, has to adhere to also. In just reading the report there were about 40 schools who applied for reaccreditation that were deferred last year for some reason. The eyes and ears are out there looking at our department from external accreditors and the accreditations commission. So, that I think really will provide national credibility in the future, and it gets our name out on the table with other peer institutions from all across the country.

The same assessment and reporting tools and criteria that are used to measure student success during the time they are working toward their degrees can likewise be used to longitudinally measure the effectiveness of the education or courses on students' success post-graduation. Many departments included in this study reported using technology to keep track of alumni, to provide access to employers, and to track the long-term success of their graduates.

Other departments reported using technology to help guide new program development by predicting what types of jobs and salaries students can and will receive and their chances of securing positions. A chair of a math and science department told us:

> Well, you've got to get that information back to the people who are going to do things differently or do things better. They collect all the information from all those surveys and reports. We may see from our employer surveys and our graduate surveys that we do get good information.

The chair of an industrial studies department at a regional public university spoke of the need to use technology to gather data about alumni:

> The goal is to go a step further and maybe do a similar kind of thing, you know, with the alums, but at the point in time that a former student is working for a company . . . and we get that information from the alums. At this point, we haven't really done that. So the challenge . . . is somehow to get that information back into the process of looking at curriculum and program in individual courses.

Develop a Plan for Resource Allocation

One of the most problematic aspects of technology for the department chair is the allocation of resources. The cost of maintaining existing technology and responding to emerging technological trends can be a significant challenge. One of the newer aspects of the chair's role is the need to assess the demand and to support the deployment of technology. Chairs must weigh the costs and benefits of technology when allocating scarce departmental resources.

As more instructional technology becomes available, departments within colleges and universities are being encouraged or pressured to add online coursework and distance education options to respond to shifting student desire for increased flexibility of anytime/anywhere instructional delivery. The increasing demand for technology-related resources in terms of currency and accessibility can be problematic unless planned for in advance and handled carefully. A chair who works at a state university expressed anxiety over the struggle to keep the department updated technologically:

> Just because technology is constantly changing and the technology doesn't come cheap, and when you get more students you need, of course, more equipment, you need more access, you need more things available to students. It affects me through what I do to keep that going without losing too much from other areas that also need to be funded. Of course computer equipment, hardware and software are expensive to keep up to date.

As would be expected, some disciplines are affected more heavily by technology than others. At the same time there are few, if any, that can avoid the impacts of technology altogether. Students, faculty, and staff expect to be connected electronically and to have seamless access to information. Department chairs are increasingly aware of the need to have a plan for technology and for the related faculty professional development that can be anticipated as technology adoption becomes a reality. Efforts to support faculty, both in terms of infrastructure and professional development, are not inexpensive but, at the same time, there is a growing recognition of the need for faculty to become and stay technologically current. Chairs in this study articulated an awareness of the institutional cost of technology hardware and software and the implications those expenditures have on the discretionary budget. A community college science department chair said:

> It is important to have a plan. We have a three-year plan for technology. We have to develop short-term, long-term, and intermediate goals, and what our needs

will be as far as technology is concerned over the next three years.

Technology has also improved the decision-making process within departments. Accessibility has created a new pool of information that is used to make decisions about the department, college, or university with more current information.

Adopt Emerging Technologies Prudently

New and emerging technologies are being introduced into teaching and research on a continual basis. Increasing numbers of faculty rely on technology to teach in the traditional classroom setting, and many are experimenting with blended courses that incorporate technology as an integral part of instruction. This often implies reduced seat time models that move away from the traditional Carnegie definition of credit hour/faculty–student contact. New uses and forms available to faculty are on the rise and can be expected to present a whole new set of issues for department chairs. A chair with 16 years of experience at a community college described the increased use of instructional technology in this way:

> What I've seen is our faculty using more technology in the classroom, both in terms of preparing the students for their clinical activities and also in terms of their teaching delivery and the interface with students. We are adding the equipment to teach with technology at a relatively rapid rate now.

Many on-campus courses now incorporate technology-based course management systems. Faculty increasingly use courseware products such as WebCT and Blackboard to support or augment instruction. It is rare to find faculty today who do not use some form of technology, even if it is nothing more than a word processor for creating notes, a web browser to access library resources or an overhead projector, and PowerPoint to deliver a lecture. At the same time, there is an increasing number of faculty who are actively exploring more sophisticated and complex uses of technology in areas such as online testing, podcasting, blogging, wikis, and visualization. This expanded use of technology by faculty will inherently place added demands on department chairs to understand the technology needs of their faculty and to work to obtain the resources to meet those needs. At a different level, the increased use of technology presents other tangential issues and challenges for faculty and chairs in areas such as workload. Just as technology offers a wide range of opportunities, it inherently carries with it concomitant challenges. While noting the advantages of technology in instruction, a chemistry chair at a large state university talked about demands on faculty created as a result of technology integration:

> There are a lot of people in the world who will sell you a bill of goods in saying, "If you just use my computer program, teaching will be easier." Hard work on a computer program or hard work on a book will educate. What we find is if we use low tech, like hand building models first, then do high tech, such as using the computer visualization second, it works great and is more time efficient for students and faculty. It isn't less work. So sometimes it's sold as less work and that's a mistake. It does make things better but it's not less work.

It will become increasingly important for chairs to understand the expectations of students as well as the expectations for technology use among faculty when discussing technology and teaching and when formulating departmental directions. While, clearly, technology can be viewed as adding to faculty workloads, it also must be recognized for the increased value it can bring to the instructional experience and for the expanded opportunities for increased information access and knowledge creation it offers both faculty and students.

Consider the Impact on Student Services

Technology has also created an increased availability of student services. Most schools today provide students with e-services through some form of portal. Today's students are able to gain access to more information more easily. It is common for students to be able to access their classes, grades, financial aid, billing information, and so on with a click of a mouse. Similarly, students on many campuses have wireless access to courses, the library, email, and social software throughout campus. A community college chair stated:

> You know, students can go in and access their schedules and the school calendar and what courses are being offered and look up their transcripts and personal information and faculty can go in and do that same stuff. It affects being able to help students with enrollment. It affects overriding them into classes.

Department chairs are clearly faced with a changing world that is increasingly being defined by technology. While technology-related issues are increasingly complex and problematic, most chairs are finding it necessary to embrace the growing opportunities that technology provides for their departments, faculty, and students. As has often been said, when the genie is out of the bottle it is very hard to put it back. As more faculty use technology to support their research and to deliver and improve their teaching and student learning, and as new generations of technology-connected students arrive on campus, chairs can expect to spend more of their time dealing with technology-related issues. The technology genie is clearly out of the bottle.

Conclusion

This chapter has described the unique challenges and opportunities that chairs encounter as they consider the ways and means of incorporating accessible, appropriate, effective, and affordable technologies into traditional teaching, research, and service functions of their departments. Charting a course for technology integration has, in recent years, become a major task of chairs. As you contemplate your strategy for dealing with technology in your department, you might wish to consider the following questions:

- Are we clear about our intended outcomes and how technology can assist in achieving these ends?
- What investments must we make to increase our effectiveness and efficiency in teaching, research, and outreach?
- What training needs to be available to faculty and staff to meet continuing technology improvements?
- How does a chair develop the knowledge needed to make good decisions about the use of technology? What other resources are available to help make those decisions, and do we have criteria that we can use to help us decide what technologies to use?
- Do we have a plan for implementing and sustaining technology in the department?
- Do we have success measures that we can use to demonstrate the effectiveness of our use of specific technologies?

Endnotes

1. The following organizational web pages were last located at the respective URLs listed:

   - Teaching, Learning, and Technology Group: www.tltgroup.org/
   - Flashlight Project: www.tltgroup.org/flashlightP.htm
   - MERLOT: www.merlot.org/
   - Western Cooperative for Educational Telecommunications (WCET): www.wcet.info/home.asp
   - Roadmap to Redesign: www.center.rpi.edu/R2R.htm

- National Center for Academic Transformation:
  www.center.rpi.edu/index.html

- Sloan Foundation: www.sloan.org/main.shtml

Suggested Resources

Brown, D. G. (Ed.). (2003). *Ubiquitous computing: The universal use of computers on college campuses*. Bolton, MA: Anker.

This is an interesting and useful work that looks at the growing phenomenon of the laptop university. While some universities are formally adopting required laptop strategies, virtually all will be affected to a greater or lesser degree by students who expect to be able to engage learning on their own terms within the context of mobile and portable technologies.

Duderstadt, J. J., Atkins, D. E., & Van Houweling, D. (2002). *Higher education in the digital age: Technology issues and strategies for American colleges and universities*. Westport, CT: Praeger.

This excellent book looks at the use of technology in higher education. The authors not only discuss the instructional and research uses of technology but also place technology within the institutional context and explore the impact that technology has on the institutional environment itself. Like other authors who have explored the intersection of technology and higher education, Duderstadt et al. suggest that institutions must change as a result of technology. Moreover, they highlight the importance of leadership in leveraging this technology.

Howe, N., & Strauss, W. (2000). *Millennials rising: The next great generation*. New York, NY: Vintage.

This is one of two books that looks at the technology implications of students entering college in the new millennium. This book, and one edited by Oblinger and Oblinger (2005), are essential reading for department chairs. Students of the 21st century are coming to college with very different expectations for technology, which will demand and force changes in how faculty teach, how institutions provide service, and how we construct the social and learning opportunities we offer our students.

Oblinger, D. G., & Oblinger, J. L. (Eds.). (2005). *Educating the net generation*. Boulder, CO: EDUCAUSE.

Diana and James Oblinger provide an excellent glimpse into today's students, those they call the "Net Generation." The book describes students who have grown up immersed in technology and who see technology as an integral part of their lives and expect it to serve them. This book provides a unique look at today's students who are "always connected," who view learning as a social and collaborative activity, and who expect access to information resources anytime and anywhere, thus posing new and unique challenges for higher education.

Weigel, V. B. (2001). *Deep learning for a digital age: Technology's untapped potential to enrich higher education*. San Francisco, CA: Jossey-Bass.

Weigel provides a very useful resource that explores technology integration and helps the reader understand some of the pedagogical underpinnings of the use of technology in teaching. Particularly useful for the department chair are several practical examples that show how technology can help improve learning outcomes.

11

Adapt to Funding and Resources Challenges

There's more and more pressure on publicly funded institutions to support themselves with the dwindling state funds, and so the department will need to continue to work on extramural funding [and] creating other more creative ways of funding itself.
                    —*A chair at a regional university*

A 2004 article in *The Chronicle of Higher Education* described public higher education as facing the "perfect storm" characterized by shrinking state appropriations and soaring demands that continue to widen the gap between institutional needs and available resources (Conklin & Reindl, 2004). Institutions are facing increased costs, declining budgets, and taxpayer and governmental demands to limit tuition and fees. At the same time they face calls for greater access, improved outcomes, and increased accountability.

This chapter explores how the current financial environment is affecting departments and suggests strategies that chairs can use to attract, maximize, and leverage available resources. As you proceed through the following material, we suggest that you keep in mind the following questions:

- What discretionary resources are at your disposal through the normal budgetary processes of the college and institution?

- What opportunities exist to increase grants, fund-raising (development), and entrepreneurial activities?
- How can you align departmental goals with college or institutional goals to identify additional funding opportunities?
- Are you familiar with the procedures for requesting new or additional instructional or research funds?
- Are you familiar with the procedures for requesting new or additional funds for professional development?
- What interdepartmental or interdisciplinary grants are available from the college or institution?
- What opportunities exist for collaboration with external agencies?
- What nonmonetary strategies can you use to reward and incent your faculty?

Public support for and treatment of universities are changing. Where once institutions were "state supported," they are increasingly becoming "state assisted," or simply "state located." Likewise, private institutions, despite arguably strong economic times nationally, face increasing budgetary pressure as competition for students and demands to diversify revenue streams become more intense.

Responding to the fiscal and political realities, higher education administrators increasingly develop institutional budgets, strategies, and policies designed ultimately to gain operational efficiencies by "doing more with less." They also engage in aggressive efforts designed to enhance revenue through public/private partnerships and collaborations, increased soft money (research productivity), and expansion of development (gifts).

Clarify Responsibility for Budget Development and Allocation

Many taxonomies have been offered to describe the various roles of department chairs (Carroll & Gmelch, 1994; Creswell, Wheeler, Seagren, Egly, & Beyer, 1990; Lucas, 1994, 2000; McLaughlin, Montgomery, & Malpass, 1975; Tucker, 1992). While each of these models approaches the chair's role from a different perspective, at some level they all serve to describe activities in one of three general spheres: academic, administrative, and leadership, with the administrative function most often encompassing some element of budget/resource management or fiscal responsibility. Whereas the role of the chair involved with budget management is more explicit when thinking in terms of the administrative role of the department chair, the management of resources (including budget management) is implicit whether viewing the chair role as an "enabler" or "provider" in the sense of being a facilitator (Creswell & Brown, 1992).

Regardless of the institutional strategies adopted, chairs find themselves carrying the academic flag or banner on the front line of the fiscal battlefield. Charged with providing discipline-level leadership, chairs have the ultimate responsibility for academic delivery while at the same time enjoying varying degrees of control over the budgets and resources that define what a department and faculty can accomplish. Gmelch and Burns (1993) identified several areas of stress for department chairs. Of the top 10 stressors related to time pressure, "obtaining program approval and financial support" (54%) was second only to "heavy workload" (59%).

As we look at funding and resources within the context of department chair leadership, it is also interesting to note that the role of the chair in fiscal matters is not necessarily clear cut. In a recent study of department chair preparation conducted at the University of Nevada–Las Vegas, a divergence of opinion about the chair's role in the management of budgetary resources was evident. Department chairs identified budgetary issues as one of the three primary areas of concern, along with personnel management and balancing roles.

Interestingly, when deans were similarly asked to identify areas of importance to the success of department chairs, budget and resource management was downplayed. While chairs saw budget and resource management as an important element, deans tended to hold the view that "budgets are fixed, handed down to the chairs with little opportunity to add resources or move money around." The view of deans appears to be that budget management at the department level is little more than an accounting function (Wolverton, Ackerman, & Holt, 2005).

It is interesting to note, however, that most research involving the roles of department chairs includes providing or managing funding and resources as one of the tasks that consume their time and attention. Regardless of the actual amount of budgetary discretion that chairs have in reality, when asked about their preparedness to handle budget management issues, the majority of chairpersons responding to the UNLV study reported being inadequately prepared and, from their perspective, budget management was clearly one of their responsibilities.

While institutional practice varies (depending on structure, policy, collective bargaining, governance, etc.), chairs generally have a reasonable degree of direct control over and responsibility for the budgets that affect the direct operations of their departments (i.e., discretionary budgets for travel, professional development, and office-level support such as copying, phones, and materials). Moreover, in an administrative leadership capacity, they also have the ability to exert varying levels of influence or indirect control on policy and budgetary decisions through interactions with other chairpersons within their college and with deans as decisions are made that affect the direction or position of the college and, hence, the department (Tucker, 1984).

At the department level (and beyond the political advocacy role in promoting and representing the interests of the department at the college and institutional level), chairs generally allocate financial resources and respond to budget constraints in one of two ways: through measures designed to achieve cost containment and through strategies that rely on a combination of leadership, flexibility, and creativity.

Interviews conducted with chairs as part of the study conducted for this *Handbook* highlighted several approaches to cost containment that were voluntarily adopted by chairpersons to increase departmental flexibility or were used by chairs in response to mandatory constraints imposed at the college or institutional level:

- Balancing the use of tenure-track and adjunct faculty
- Management of delivery factors (e.g., differentiated workload, credit hour production, class reassignment, class release)
- Deferral of maintenance (e.g., technology, labs, teaching environments)
- Strategic use of early retirements
- Restriction on discretionary travel
- Salary freezes
- Expanded use of graduate students or peer-level activities (i.e., peer advising)

Department chairs likewise described the use of several alternative strategies to address budgetary constraints that exhibit varying degrees of leadership, innovation, and creativity. For example:

- Strategic use of one-time funds available at the college or institutional level
- Direct requests or advocacy to the dean for special projects
- Reallocation of funds between personnel and other categories
- Fostering a positive tone within the department
- Reliance on programmatic strategies that focus on growth
- Cultivation of local and regional collaborations
- Targeted use of supplemental pay (stipends, merit pay, etc.)

In an interesting conference paper that highlighted the importance of chairperson support for faculty professional development, particularly in times of financial constraints or cutbacks, Mott (1994) amplified the importance of faculty morale. She underscored the leadership dimension of the chair's role and the need to work creatively to identify resources and to provide department members with encouragement, support, and a sense of purpose. The connection between morale and departmental resources and funding is addressed later in this chapter.

To better understand how chairs view and respond to several of the funding and resource management issues previously identified, it is useful to look at how chairs describe the implications of these issues and how they respond as they seek to guide their departmental efforts. In what follows we explore several key areas from the chair perspective to gain a broader appreciation of how funding and resource issues influence department chair leadership thinking and action.

Recognize the Implications of Budget Pressures

As previously noted, there are different opinions about the importance of a chairperson's budget management responsibilities, depending on the administrative perspective (dean versus chair). What is not in question, however, is the recognition of the impact that budgetary constraints have on the institutional environment at all levels, including the department. When asked about budget pressures and how they manifest themselves at the department level, chairs articulated a common theme. A physics chair at a mid-sized institution responded, "We have to be very conscious of budgets and how we're going to allocate our monies to make sure we can continue to support evolving technologies."

When asked about the challenges that chairs are facing in today's higher education environment, several respondents expressed the increasing demand to support programs or departments in light of diminishing state or institutional funds. A chair at a mid-sized regional public university responded, "The resources [are] declining and no matter how wealthy or affluent [institutions] become, I think the amount of resources we need to run a good, sound educational institution [is] declining."

Tight institutional budgets and declining state support can have profound impacts on institutions. Following the 2005 devastation wreaked upon New Orleans by hurricanes Katrina and Rita, major reductions in state funding of higher education were unavoidable. The impacts included the reduction of merit-based aid, suspension of program development, deferral of maintenance, and reduction in staff and faculty (Fischer, 2005). While Louisiana probably represents a worst-case scenario, state spending on higher education between 2000 and 2005 reflected the poor financial conditions of many states. In 2004–2005 only 14 states increased higher education funding by 5% or more (Fischer, 2006). Despite a more positive trend recorded in 2005–2006, revenues in the last few years have generally failed to keep pace with costs driven by increased demands for access, programs, and services. In the face of fiscal reality, higher education institutions have found it necessary to reduce budgets, increase tuition, seek alternative funding, and slow the pace of growth.

As chairpersons struggle to respond to the realities of ever-increasing costs and declining institutional budgets, inevitably they are faced with having to balance budgets, delivery and offerings, and quality as department activities vie for limited resources. The need both to respond to budgetary realities and to ensure quality is clearly an issue faced by many chairs. At the same time, chairs are not particularly optimistic that funding at the department level will improve in the near future, despite the more positive economic outlook projected for 2006 and beyond by the federal government. As the chair of an honors program at a two-year college commented, "As we're dealing with faculty and students we want quality instruction as well as quality materials, and I think everyone has experienced financial difficulties in the last couple of years, and I don't foresee that letting up anytime soon." One of the best expressions of the position that chairs find themselves in was made by a chair at a Canadian college:

> Choose what you're going to do and be better than anybody else, but don't water it down. I think . . . it has been a big, big issue, particularly the last few years and I think that's going to continue. But the trend then is what dominates the motivation in postsecondary education and where the business model becomes more dominant than education or the student experience. I think that [education] gets relegated to a position of irrelevance, certainly at some level in discussions. [The chair] kind of gets caught.

However, for many chairpersons, budget reductions have already taken a significant toll. A chair of an anthropology department at a large research institution expressed his frustration by commenting, "We're at the point where you're cutting substance, and how do you cut substance and still maintain your reputation, your excellence. It's a horrible kind of decision you have to make." Nonetheless, chairs, on the whole, appear to be realistic about future financial prospects, while at the same time are unwilling to compromise in the delivery of quality education. This theme was echoed by many of the chairs with whom we spoke. For example, a chair who has led an arts department for nine years commented on repeated budget reductions from the legislature:

> The challenge is to balance what you believe to be the right thing. What's being dominated it seems or what's dominating educational decisions at a higher level is budget, and this chase for full-time students or motivation for more numbers, bigger numbers, and it's [all about] resisting that and still maintaining high standards in what you do.

Diversify Funding Through Revenue Generation Strategies

As funding from general or common sources becomes tighter, successful organizations tend to become more aggressive and creative in identifying and attracting alternative sources of revenue. At the institutional level these efforts often become strategic priorities and include major initiatives to increase grant productivity, redouble efforts in the area of development (gifts), include the initiation of major capital campaigns, promote entrepreneurial efforts, and expand enrollment. As the effects of budget reductions trickle down from the institutional level to the college and department levels, similar efforts to tap into alternative funding sources are evident.

By virtue of the operational nature of their administrative roles, chairs are more directly affected by budget reductions, institutional and college initiatives, and policy decisions that emanate from senior administrators. Moreover, it is that direct operational aspect of dealing with budgets that creates the incentive for the chair to explore a variety of strategies to deal with the reality of scarce resources. As one chair at a public college described it:

> Well, I think [that] budgetarily there's more and more pressure on publicly funded institutions to support themselves with the dwindling state funds and so the department will need to continue to work on extramural funding [and] creating other more creative ways of funding itself.

The expectation that chairpersons will work more aggressively to identify and attract additional resources needed by their departments was articulated by a chair at a regional four-year public institution when he described his efforts to augment the department budget: "We're constantly working with our resource people and our grants division to see if there's other money available. We're constantly looking for money, just to supplement what we need."

The breadth of strategies adopted by chairs to respond to the resource needs of their departments was documented in a study conducted at the community college level (Miller, Benton, & Vacik, 1998). Using a Delphi technique, the researchers worked with a group of department chairs to identify 40 strategies for managing scarce resources or maintaining quality programs. Among the strategies that gained the broadest agreement were collaboration or sharing of resources, management of course offerings (course rotation), focus on critical program elements, program evaluation, streamlining or elimination of noncritical activities, communication of reductions to department members, identification and elimination of waste, leveraging faculty strengths, building relationships with external businesses and agencies, use of instructional contracts to generate revenue, and increased reliance on part-time personnel.

Recent interviews conducted as part of the research for this *Handbook* confirmed or expanded on several of the strategies just identified. Themes that were mentioned repeatedly included the following:

- One-time funding and use of reserves
- Proposals designed to enhance or grow programs
- Focus on grants (both internal and external)
- Collaborations and consortia
- Development (fund-raising)
- Alumni relationship management
- Revenue-generating contracts
- Program and department advocacy

Regardless of the industry, one of the interesting aspects of budgeting and fiscal management is the creation of one-time funds and/or reserves that come about as operational spending falls short of planned expenditures. And while this delta between budget and spending occurs in every enterprise, higher education tends to generate and rely on these one-time funds to address priorities that were not included in the operational budget or to provide start-up money for new initiatives or proposals.

One-time funding and accumulated reserves are generally controlled at the highest levels of the administration and are allocated downward through the organization based on identified needs, proposals, and initiatives that gain visibility. Assertive chairpersons can position their departments to take advantage of this one-time funding source, particularly to support new initiatives and spur growth. Likewise, reserves that are accumulated can be used subsequently to soften the impact of tighter financial conditions. A chair of a music department at a large state university described the positive impact of reserves in this way:

> There's been some really good management on our campus in the surplus years. Previous years the president was able to sock away the funds so the reduction, at least for this year, has not really affected us greatly to any degree. In fact, it's negligible; we haven't really felt it.

While the use of reserves tends to be a more general institutional strategy that can level year-to-year fiscal variations due to changes in funding, annual accumulations of one-time money are more targeted and can be an intermittent source of department resources. Chairpersons can leverage these windows of funding opportunity to augment operational budgets. A chair at a prominent community college stated:

> We have the opportunity at the end of the year to do what's called additional allocations, so if there is any money left over within the college itself, we can request to have spending for things that we may need that we didn't know and didn't plan for accordingly. So there's actually quite a few avenues, unfortunately, not enough to do everything all at once, but usually to keep everything afloat.

One-time funds are particularly useful when departments engage in formal (or semiformal) planning processes that result in an articulated direction or set of program or project priorities. Senior administration is more likely to fund a proposal that is aligned with the strategic direction of the institution and that is part of a defined and planned direction. The importance of having a definitive plan when seeking one-time or opportunity funding was best articulated by a chair at a regional state institution:

> The strategic initiative with the college this size has money they set aside out of the budget. It's kind of like a pot of money where there's feeder money to do something. You take ideas, you get your money, and you build on that. The college puts the money out and they know it's a risk, but a lot of good ideas have come out of that, a lot of good programs.

As state support for higher education has declined relative to increasing expenditure levels, institutional leadership has turned its attention to private giving as a source of funding. As these efforts become more sophisticated, the increased focus on fund-raising (often termed *development*) engages the entire campus community from the president down to the faculty. Whether the private gifts come from individuals, alumni, or private foundations, they play an increasingly important role in institutional operations.

Chairpersons who embrace development efforts and who can enlist the support of their faculty for fund-raising activities can often attract supplemental funding. Well-defined development efforts can provide supplemental revenue streams that can be used to fund scholarships, support labs, augment research, fund endowed faculty lines, and so on. As the chair of a science department at a mid-sized institution commented:

> The financial pressure [here] is perhaps less than it is at some other places. The leadership of the president and the business office and the alumni and development

office has centered on fund-raising and it has kept the
focus of the academic departments. We are trying to
develop revenue streams within the department in terms
of our supporting our labs, our research labs.

While many chairs undoubtedly shy away from active fund-raising for a variety of reasons, the potential should not be ignored or
downplayed. Effective fund-raising efforts can attract resources that
have a significant impact on a department. As a chair at a mid-sized
public university, who actively engaged in successful fund-raising
activities, put it: "It has allowed us to bring in over $1.2 million in
external funding, so it's been a terrific, terrific partnership and a relation with the community that's helped us in every way possible."

Successful chairs often turn to grant writing or entrepreneurial
activities as a source for supplemental departmental funding. Grant
opportunities can be found both within the institution and externally through a variety of public and private grant funding agencies
and organizations. Although grant funding opportunities tend to be
more prevalent or lucrative for some disciplines (e.g., the sciences,
business, or education), most can attract some level of supplemental grant funding. In the words of a performing arts chair at a four-
year public university:

And so the joke has been for the last 20 to 25 years that
we have gone from a state-supported institution to a
state-located institution. Actual [operational] monies
that we have are supplied by the state. The rest of the
money is supplied by our own institution in an entrepreneurial fashion. But the college also has a grant program, an internal grant program that is reasonably
well-funded so our folk[s] here can apply for these various grants.

Similarly, departments in certain disciplines tend to have
increased opportunities to engage in entrepreneurial or contract
activities. These, however, can be time consuming, as a chair of a

music program at a private college pointed out: "Well, my challenge has been developing contracts with outside agencies or curriculum for outside profit or nonprofit groups. I spent often more time on that side than the academic side and that was always a challenge."

Capitalize on Changes in Staffing

A 1999 study conducted by the Higher Education Research Institute at the University of California–Los Angeles found that roughly one third of full-time faculty teaching in the United States are 55 years of age or older.[1] Most individuals who assume the role of chairperson in the first decade of the 21st century will face the issue of increasing numbers of faculty retirements. One chair at an urban university spoke for most of his peers when he remarked, "I am worried about the graying of the academy and who we're going to find to replace people."

Not only does this graying of the professoriate have interesting cultural, organizational, professional, programmatic, and interpersonal dimensions, it presents chairs with both challenges and opportunities when recruiting new faculty and leveraging salary savings derived from the salary differential that most often occurs between the departing and the incoming faculty. As a concerned chair of philosophy at a two-year school observed:

> One of the things we're faced with, our department is just very recently getting to the point where we have more new people than we have senior. When I was chair we were probably 80% full professors and now we're about half and half and so now we've got all this training to do with the mentoring that we need for these people. That's going to be a huge job. Too many new people and not enough of us old-timers left to do it.

On the positive side, chairs who exert leadership and articulate a departmental vision can use the replacement of retiring faculty and the recruitment process to foster new program interest and to help shape the departmental direction. In addition, it is often possible for the chairperson to make a case for the retention and reinvestment of the salary savings to further grow programs, provide released time to address grant writing, jump-start entrepreneurial efforts, or enhance teaching and learning through faculty professional development.

Although institutions, colleges, and departments prefer to think in terms of growth through the expansion of existing programs or the development of new ones, fiscal realities can sometimes result in hard choices. Chairs who face difficult decisions as a result of reduced budgets might need to consider using retirement as a means of cost cutting. A chair with 17 years of experience at a large public university, facing the prospect of ongoing budget reductions, shared this thought:

> I think in the next three to five years [the] budget will continue to play a dominant role. I think that one of the challenges will be to create some kind of dialogue and understanding that if a faculty member retires they [are] not going to be replaced.

Because personnel costs represent the largest portion of most departmental budgets, budget reductions can be particularly problematic. While a reduction of faculty (typically accompanied by the expanded use of adjuncts) is not something that most chairpersons want to do, the use of pending retirements is often more palatable to the remaining faculty than are cuts in faculty professional development, equipment, travel, or support for grant writing or research.

Maintain High Morale During Trying Times

The final dimension of dealing with funding and resource allocation (particularly in times of forced reductions) is the issue of faculty and departmental morale. The availability of resources rarely serves to create high sustained morale levels; however, lack of adequate resources or forced budget reductions have the potential to cause a serious problem with morale.

Several strategies for dealing with faculty morale during times of diminishing resources were offered by Halford (1994) in an interesting conference paper. A study of 25 institutions in 13 states identified 9 variables related to professional self-esteem that contribute to faculty effectiveness and morale. The study identified physical environment, consultative management, open communication, honesty and evenhandedness, open budgetary process, classroom control, adequate support services, opportunity for professional growth and renewal, and involvement in establishing the institutional mission, goals, and objectives as the key elements affecting morale. While some of these factors do not have direct financial or resource implications, effective management of available resources by the chairperson can contribute to a positive and supportive environment.

The study described two other significant factors that contribute to positive faculty morale over which chairs can exert some degree of influence: enhanced self-esteem and shared departmental governance. The chair can contribute to the faculty member's sense of self-esteem through direct interaction and the recognition of the faculty member's contributions and importance to the department's overall well-being and future. Likewise, open and honest communication, participation in departmental governance, opportunities for personal and professional growth, and reasonable levels of support for faculty efforts (all of which have some tangential relationship to resource allocation) can make a significant difference in the morale of the department. As much as effective management of resources is about simple good business practices for the chairperson, it is also about setting a positive tone, articulating a collective vision, and supporting those things that are valued by the faculty both individually and collectively. A chair of a communications department at a regional university summed up this juncture between the business and resource aspects and the morale-building aspects of the chair's job when she said, "You have to keep momentum, certainly. If we can maintain [and] sustain a quality program, that's what I think we have, and as well the morale of the faculty. That'll be a good accomplishment."

Depending on the institutional environment, chairs will have various degrees of discretion in managing or guiding funding and resource allocation. What is important to remember is that actual amounts of direct control are less important than the effective use of that control in setting and supporting a tone and direction that engenders trust in the process and positive faculty feeling.

The more discretion chairpersons have in managing departmental resources, the more assertive they can be in establishing and promoting a vibrant and dynamic departmental tone. Nonetheless, chairs should not underestimate the impact that they can have to garner resources for their departments through effective advocacy. The chair of a history department at a public university described that aspect of his job when he said:

> I guess I would say that I think I've been fairly influential inside and outside the department and I suppose that is something that has developed over the three years by gaining people's confidence, both in the department and in the college and university administrations.

At the same time, chairs must face reality and accept that not all decisions are going to be popular and that they will be criticized from time to time. The chair of a business department had this hard-won advice to offer other chairs:

> You have to accept the role and it's going to cause some of those tensions and some of those frustrations or anxieties around it, and you just have to have the confidence and the strength to realize that it's not always going to work out and everyone isn't going to love you.

Conclusion

This chapter has provided a description of the present state of higher education with respect to funding, and it highlighted the budgetary pressures being felt by nearly all colleges and universities, regardless of location, size, or mission. The chapter offered several strategies that chairs can consider as they work to diversify revenue streams (such as grants, development and fund-raising, collaborations and consortia, and entrepreneurship). Finally, it chronicled the changing nature of today's faculty and offered several approaches that chairs can use to maintain the morale of their faculty in the face of limited budgets and resources.

As you confront the challenges of using existing resources efficiently and securing new resources, you might wish to ask yourself the following questions:

- Do you have a sufficient understanding of the financial and budgetary processes of your institution to identify and take advantage of funding opportunities?
- How do you encourage faculty participation in the generation of new revenue streams through activities such as fund-raising, entrepreneurship, and grantsmanship? What can you do to encourage and support those efforts?
- Does your departmental direction support the strategic direction of the institution, and how can you leverage that synergy to garner needed resources?
- Have you developed a departmental culture that allows you to effectively engage in interdepartmental, interdisciplinary, and interinstitutional collaborations and consortia?

Endnotes

1. The American College Teacher (University of California–Los Angeles, Higher Education Research Institute, 1999), last viewed at www.gseis.ucla.edu/heri/heri.html.

Suggested Resources

Barr, M. J. (2002). *Jossey-Bass academic administrator's guide to budgets and financial management*. San Francisco, CA: Jossey-Bass.

> This publication provides an excellent initial overview of the budget for a new chair or administrator. It discusses the role of the unit budget, including sources of funding support, the purposes of the budget and the amount of the budget, the budget cycle, the pitfalls and problems identified by unit administrators and how to avoid them, and strategies for addressing budget reductions.

Jones, D. (2006). *State shortfalls projected to continue despite economic gains: Long-term prospects for higher education no brighter*. San Jose, CA: National Center for Public Policy and Higher Education.

> This publication provides an excellent overview of the current higher education environment relative to funding. Jones, who has conducted extensive research in higher education policy, paints a picture of the future prospects for funding of higher education that suggests continued constraints on public funding.

Lees, N. D. (2006). *Chairing academic departments: Traditional and emerging expectations*. Bolton, MA: Anker.

> This book is an excellent resource that chairs will want to add to their collections. The author provides fresh insights into several key aspects relating to the role of chairs and offers practical advice and strategies to respond to today's demands.

Miller, M. T., Benton, C. J., & Vacik, S. M. (1998, April–May). Managing scarce resources in the community college: Strategies for the department chair. *Community College Journal of Research and Practice, 22*(3), 203–211.

> Few chairs feel that they have all of the resources they need or would like to have. This is a practical guide that offers suggestions for managing scarce resources. The article contains strategies to address such issues as staffing, workload assignment, program quality, and so on.

Mott, M. (1994, February). *The hunt for hidden resources: A chair's guide to finding campus support for faculty and staff development*. Paper presented at the 3rd International Conference for Community College Chairs, Deans, and Other Instructional Leaders, Phoenix, AZ.

> This document provides a useful resource for chairs as they look for alternative funding sources to augment base funding. The author offers several useful suggestions and strategies that can be used to identify resources that might otherwise be overlooked.

Shaw, R. (1995). Fund raising—An essential activity for all undergraduate department chairs. *Journal of College Science Teaching, 24*(5), 308.

This resource addresses the importance of fund-raising for chairs. As public funding for higher education becomes scarcer, chairs are more often finding themselves in the position of having to look for resources from alternative sources. This article provides a good foundation for thinking about this fund-raising role.

12

Foster a Culture of
Continuous Improvement

*Our job as leaders is to inspire and excite people with
the vision of where we could be and what we could be
together. And that takes energy every day to be there.
They have to know that you are there for them.*
                    —A chair of a business department

In the Preface to this edition of the *Handbook*, we pointed out
that, in addition to the perennial issues chairs face in administering their departments, they must now confront the difficult task
of addressing issues of access, affordability, quality, and accountability. It is therefore appropriate that, as we near the end of this
guide to chairing academic departments, we return to these issues
and provide advice about how to respond to these forces of change
in higher education. The issue today is not whether to provide
greater access with the same or fewer resources or whether to
improve quality and results but, rather, how to accomplish these
challenging goals.

> Higher education has a well-deserved reputation for sta-
> bility over the decades, even over the centuries. Despite
> this, change is already happening. Several factors make
> staying the same unlikely. Within the policy worlds, both
> state and federal, there is rising concern about the need

to address critical issues that affect the performance of higher education. (Newman, Couturier, & Scurry, 2004, p. 198)

Following nearly a quarter of a century of experimenting with, initially, Total Quality Management (TQM) and, more recently, Continuous Quality Improvement (CQI), higher education has distilled the essence from these various quality movements and adapted their methods and metrics to the unique operation of academic institutions. The quality movement has caused institutions to become far more intentional and systematic in the design and delivery of their curricula and far more diligent in measuring the results of what they say they do and what they actually do.

The area of quality improvement and assessment has become increasingly important in recent years, and interest in it by policymakers, the public, accrediting bodies, boards of governors, and other political leaders shows no signs of abating. Accrediting bodies recommend and, more commonly, require an emphasis on continuous improvement in conjunction with assessment processes designed to help schools and departments develop and measure learning outcomes. This is an area where chairpersons can exhibit valuable leadership on behalf of their departments. As you read through this chapter, you might wish to reflect on the following questions:

- In what ways does your institution and department consider continuous improvement a priority?
- Are there strategies and resources to support quality improvement efforts?
- Are faculty supportive of such efforts, and, if not, how might you encourage them?
- Are there reliable assessment measures in place to track progress over time, make comparisons, and demonstrate results?

Make Continuous Improvement a Priority

The focus on continuous improvement brings us back to the diagram we talked about in the first chapter. It depicts a dramatic interplay of forces that affect chairs and their departments. At the core of the enterprise lies *learning* and *performance*, which also carry connotations of outcomes and productivity. Around these core functions of higher education are the systems, processes, and practices that departments use—and chairs lead—that ensure that they produce the desired results. Building on a base of mutual trust, departments that are open to collaboration and teamwork can lead to a deeper understanding of what they do and how they do it. Ultimately, this understanding forms the basis for improvement and assessment. Assuming the primacy of learning and performance, chairpersons must play a key role in devising ways to improve student learning. Similarly, they must foster the conditions under which departments are accountable for producing results.

Excellence or quality might be evidenced in your department in multiple ways but primarily by creating an exceptional learning environment for students and a positive work environment for faculty. It might be helpful to ask the following questions:

- What will enhance learning and increase performance on the part of students?
- What will improve the level of performance of faculty in teaching research and scholarships?
- How can we increase the overall performance of the department?
- How will we develop a reputation for programs that are recognized for excellence locally, nationally, and internationally?
- What programs will attract outside resources?

Institutions and departments that consider assessment and continuous improvement to be a priority have a palpable inquisitiveness at their core, and they are dedicated to examining their work in an

open manner and with a long-term desire to see engaged and motivated students thrive as they participate in the learning process. They
relish the opportunity to reflect on the progress students make toward
learning goals and outcomes. They consider collaborative processes
that integrate fields of knowledge with life experiences to increase
the depth of learning and connectedness among ideas and concepts.

The connectedness of learning requires departments to work
with other parts of the institution to enhance the learning process.
The integrated use of all of higher education's resources is needed
in the education and preparation of the whole student. For purposes
of this chapter we will adopt the definition of learning advanced by
the authors of *Learning Reconsidered* (Keeling, 2004) as "a comprehensive, holistic, transformative activity that integrates academic
learning and student development, processes that have often been
considered separate" (p. 2).

The authors of this joint publication of the American College
Personnel Association and the National Association of Student
Personnel Administrators state:

> We no longer believe that learning is the passive corol-
> lary of teaching, or that students do, or should, simply
> absorb material presented in lectures and textbooks. The
> new concept of *learning* recognizes the essential integra-
> tion of personal development with learning; it reflects
> the diverse ways through which students may engage, as
> whole people with multiple dimensions and unique per-
> sonal histories, with the tasks and content of learning.
> (Keeling, 2004, p. 3)

Studies reveal characteristics of departments that value continuous improvement and quality. According to Wergin (2003, p. 8),
a survey of 60 department chairs found that departments that had
the following characteristics probably value quality:

- Shared mission
- External recognition

- High academic standards
- Excellence in teaching
- Active scholarship
- Collaboration and self-reflection
- Innovation and flexibility to change
- Collegiality
- Effective communication
- Balance among students, community, institution, faculty
- A "quality" chair
- Successful students
- Adequate facilities and strong support staff
- Respect for diversity of opinion and "creative tension"

The challenge for the chair is to create a culture where innovation, quality, and results are embraced.

Devise Strategies and Resources to Support Quality Improvement Efforts

There are several resources available to a department chair in the process of continuous improvement. Accrediting bodies are one source of support designed to help schools and departments develop and measure learning outcomes. For example, the North Central Association (NCA) is currently recommending the Academic Quality Improvement Program (AQIP) process for accreditation. This process was developed utilizing the Baldrige criteria for quality as a guideline. It requires the institution to develop a mission, vision, and goals, and then to focus the process toward those goals.

One of the major shifts in the accreditation process over the past five years has been the emphasis on total institutional assessment of student learning outcomes. This change recognizes the necessity of connecting student learning with activities and life experiences outside the classroom, which enhances and deepens learning. This shift encourages academic departments to work not only with other academic departments to form linkages in learning but also to work with student life, athletic programs, campus ministries, service-learning, and other entities to enhance and deepen the learning experience. An excellent resource for understanding this concept of holistic learning is *Learning Reconsidered* (Keeling, 2004; with its obvious allusion to Boyer's influential *Scholarship Reconsidered*, 1990, another call for educational refocus).

This emphasis on institutional assessment of learning outcomes is a broadly based movement involving your peers in many other institutions. Additional support comes from the administration (the second ring of the diagram), the accrediting team, and professional organizations as you refine departmental goals and learning outcomes. Another resource is the sessions on assessment at disciplinary conferences and publications focused on assessment and learning outcomes by professional disciplinary associations. Many campuses have an individual or committee assigned to assessment or accreditation who can serve as a coach and guide in this process.

Fundamental to education is the need to evaluate student learning and the effectiveness of program design and delivery. These are the three areas of assessment (part of the inner ring on our diagram) that are vital to each academic department. Assessment allows faculty to determine how well students are learning, to fine-tune content and pedagogy, and it allows the department or division to evaluate the effectiveness of entire programs.

A chair of a humanities department at a state university put it this way: "We need to be sure we're giving students what they need, and preparing them for careers or advancement in their careers." An effective way to assure meeting these goals is to follow the three-tiered approach to assessment of student learning, teaching effectiveness, and program effectiveness.

Student Learning Assessment

A written midterm and final examination that evaluate only a student's ability to memorize and recall information is clearly inadequate in today's educational environment. Active learning curriculum objectives focus on the acquisition of knowledge and skills that will enrich students' lives outside the classroom. Students need knowledge and skills that function at a higher level than the rote learning skills that were once expected. Students need critical thinking, problem solving, communication, and human relations skills.

Ongoing classroom assessment needs to provide for continuous monitoring of student learning. Faculty need to receive ongoing feedback about their effectiveness, and students need to receive feedback on their progress and performance. Assignment of grades can be a part of the assessment process. Certainly quizzes and formal tests can be part of the ongoing assessment, but other methods of assessment should also be used to provide more accurate measurement of student learning.

In the past assessment strategies were often determined on the basis of course content, but most courses lend themselves to a variety of methods. A speech class lends itself to an assessment of oral reports and speeches. However, the same speech course could also use written assessment strategies by having students write reports on professional speakers. Students could also complete a self-evaluation of performance factors that the instructor could use for evaluation, or students could participate in learning groups by giving group speeches for assessment of both performance and relational skills. Additionally, a speech course lends itself to classroom discussions where students are invited to speak about the course material while the instructor listens to assess which students are grasping the concepts and reaching the goals and which ones need additional coaching in those concepts.

Assessment strategies are most effective when they are related to the course material and when students view them as relevant to their future careers. Assessment strategies that relate to students' work, such as portfolios or written reflective papers, can be very effective. Using simulated activities, case studies, scenarios for computer courses, keeping performance ratings or references, role-playing job interviews, holding mock trials, or giving students the opportunity to practice skills in real-world scenarios can also be effective in reinforcing learning.

Assessment strategies might influence students' final grades; however, the primary reason for assessment is improving learning rather than providing evidence for grading students. The goal of assessment is a more in-depth understanding of learning outcomes than a summative A-B-C grade allows.

Teaching Effectiveness Assessment

As we mentioned earlier in the chapter, fundamental to a continuous improvement culture is inquisitiveness about effectiveness. The major question most faculty will want to ask is: Does the assessment outcome show that students were able to meet the goals established for the course? Answers to this question will allow the faculty member to refine and design the course material for maximum learning for all students. The process of course refinement is never completed, and it needs to be continuous and ongoing.

Bain (2004) suggests that the best teachers

> have some systematic program—some more elaborate than others—to assess their own efforts and to make appropriate changes. Furthermore, because they are checking their own efforts when they evaluate students, they avoid judging them on arbitrary standards. Rather, the assessment of students flows from primary learning objectives. (p. 19)

He goes on to say that they are willing to "confront their own weaknesses and failures," they "don't blame their students for any of the difficulties they faced," and they

> had a strong sense of commitment to the academic community and not just to personal success in the classroom. They frequently worked on major curricular initiatives

and joined public conversations about how to improve teaching in the institution. . . . Fundamentally, they were learners, constantly trying to improve their own efforts to foster students' development, and never completely satisfied with what they had already achieved. (p. 20)

Bain notes that the best teachers

treat their teaching as they likely already treat their own scholarship or artistic creations, as serious and important intellectual and creative work, as an endeavor that benefits from careful observation and close analysis, from revision and refinement, and from dialogues with colleagues and the critiques of peers. Good teaching can be learned. (p. 21)

A large part of the learning is through this assessment process.

Program Effectiveness Assessment

To assess a department or program, a rubric needs to assess the degree to which the goals of the program have been achieved. This rubric should include the mission, vision, and goals of the department and then how assessment toward those goals will be measured. The assessment rubric goes beyond providing data for assessing goals.

The key components of program assessment should include: What services were delivered? Who were the services delivered to? What difference did it make with regard to desired educational outcomes? For an English program, the rubric could include how well students write and include the development of cohesive organization of the writing. For a math program, the assessment rubric could include how well students are able to grasp concepts as well as solve specific problems. At some institutions, final examinations include pieces of the rubric. Assessing the program allows departments to refine and design courses for maximum learning for students. Quality program assessment contributes to the management of student learning. This is an opportunity for critical evidence-based analyses of program strengths and weaknesses and of what steps need to be taken to improve the weaknesses.

Encourage Support of Continuous Improvement Efforts

Understanding the level of faculty support for continuous improvement in your department will assist you in leading this effort. There are several ways to discover the level of support the faculty in your department might have for continuous improvement. You can learn a great deal from studying the last program review, the evaluation of faculty work that has been done recently, and the student satisfaction data or teacher evaluation data that might already exist. How have faculty viewed the department? What suggestions for improvement have been made? What suggestions have been carried out since the document was completed? How involved are faculty in the department? How engaged are students? What have they suggested should be improved? How did faculty react to those suggestions?

You might discover that your department is deeply committed to continuous improvement and that documentation of changes and improvements in quality are readily evident. Or you might discover that program review is a rote process that was dutifully completed but that little follow through on recommendations has been made. You might find that there are many satisfied students and that your majors are increasing each year, or you might find that there is great dissatisfaction with the current program or parts of the curriculum.

If your department is actively engaged in continuous improvement, you may not need to read any further. If you see areas where deeper commitment to continuous improvement is needed, then the remainder of this chapter will be beneficial as it addresses issues related to motivating faculty to improve their performance.

Many studies demonstrate that intrinsic rewards are the most motivating. According to Wergin (2003), faculty say that what they enjoy most about their work is "contributing to my discipline, having an impact on students' lives, and the joy of learning" (p. 13). If you can tie any of these motivators to the improvement process, you will probably succeed in involving faculty in change and improvement. This might include developing assessment approaches that further the understanding of teaching for the specific discipline or demonstrating how students' lives have been affected by the work of your department and finding new pedagogical methods that assist students in their mastery of your discipline.

It might be helpful to have a discussion with your faculty regarding the reasons for doing assessment: It provides feedback, directs the efforts toward learning outcomes, demonstrates accountability, and is the basis for curriculum refinement and institutional learning.

Wergin (2003) suggests that one of the remedies for apathy among faculty is to "engage them meaningfully" (p. 20), which would include a sense of collective responsibility for decisions made and actions taken; that leadership must also encourage collective reflection that leads to organizational learning. He goes on to say that to foster faculty collaboration in support of departmental goals it might be best to first reflect on the work faculty are doing, link it to the collective expectations, and then help faculty to see how they might contribute to the collective work more meaningfully. By negotiating their values, finding evidence of excellence, and then by making meaning of that evidence, faculty can become engaged.

The principles of an engaged department as defined by Wergin (2003, pp. 63–64) are:

1. The work of the institution, defined in terms of its social compact and the collective work of its departmental units, frames the choices for the departmental work.
2. The department is guided both by the aggregate work of its member faculty and by how it adds value as a whole to the institution.
3. The work of the department provides a basis for framing the work that individual faculty members do.

4. Faculty members are guided in their choices both by how they add value to their disciplines and how they add value to the work of their departments.

5. Choices, whether made by individual faculty members or by departments as a whole, are the product of negotiation with key stakeholders.

The chair of a political science department at a state university said:

> I guess the main concern the department has about the future is to be sure we have the enrollments. That would be the one thing. This is the concern that motivates people to think about what courses we should be offering and shouldn't be offering.

Addressing quality issues can be realized by seeing that enrollments affect faculty job security. It is important to think about growing the number of majors, and that requires thinking and reflecting on ways to draw students into a program. Bringing students to your department requires thinking about what satisfies students and what they wish could be improved. In the current age of web sites and instant information, students are well aware of what the competition has to offer.

One of the valuable outcomes of building a culture focused on improved student learning and performance is that it unifies the academic process. Faculty will know what is expected and how they can contribute, which can lead to greater job satisfaction.

Adopt Reliable Assessment Measures to Track Progress Over Time, Make Comparisons, and Demonstrate Results

Excellence and quality can be measured through a wide variety of methods partly because assessment measurements must reflect the values of the department, college, or university. A recent workshop presenter reminded her audience that the goal of education is a high mean and small standard deviation. She went on to explain that the goal of education is to move the mean scores of students higher and to have fewer outliers. In other words, we want to reduce the variance to become more consistent in delivering quality learning. This is a simple concept that is key to the assessment of learning.

The first step of assessment is deciding what to measure. The following are elements of learning that can be measured: knowledge, skills, problem-solving abilities, attitudes, values, and spiritual commitment.

The key to meaningful measurement is to determine the main goals for your department and the best method to measure those goals. It might be helpful to also determine competencies that are required at the next level and assess that knowledge and those skills at the end of the courses you teach. You might choose to develop a list of the most important indicators of your success. Some departments develop dashboard measurements that they study each year as key performance indicators. Examples of these key indicators might be:

- Number of students in your major
- Student–teacher ratio for your major(s)
- Success of students on nationally normed examinations
- Placement rate of graduates
- Satisfaction of future employers/placement in graduate programs
- Student satisfaction data
- Research/publication data for faculty

These measurements are quantitative data. However, it is far more challenging to acquire and analyze qualitative data that are needed to guide the faculty's understanding of the acquisition of concepts and ideas.

Wiggins and McTighe (2006) have developed an example of a template that can be used in developing these learning outcomes and measurements:

1. Identify desired results, such as knowledge, context, big ideas, enduring understandings, and transfer of learning.
2. Determine acceptable evidence. Through performance of what authentic tasks will students demonstrate success? What other evidence will support this demonstration (e.g., journals, tests, discussions)?
3. Design appropriate learning experiences and instruction. What will students do to learn designated skills and knowledge and be able to apply them to real life situations?
4. Develop measurement/assessment devices for each desired learning outcome.

Assessment methods are being refined each year and tools are being developed that will help you to measure almost any goal for your department. There is an abundance of books, workshops, and articles on assessment, several of which are listed at the end of this chapter.

An Illustration of the Process

We conclude this chapter with an example of departmental improvement that incorporates many continuous improvement and assessment principles.

A well-known school of music was very concerned about the lack of enrollment in their opera major. They decided to use the continuous improvement model to understand the situation and to determine steps that could be taken to improve the number of students enrolled in their discipline. They called a department meeting and talked about what they felt were the most important values that needed to be part of the curriculum for opera majors. They then developed a list of activities that they believed would lead to improvement in their program. Next they appointed a team to find out what was being done at several other music schools. They had always been the best opera program and could not believe that other schools were surpassing them in enrollment. They discovered that other schools were designing the curriculum to include hands-on experience beginning in the freshman year. They then decided that they should have several focus groups to determine stakeholder expectations. They met with several opera companies that employed their graduates, and they also met with current students and alumni. They discovered that students preferred the immediate opera experience that other schools were offering and that opera companies found the graduates of those schools to be better informed and more adaptable to current practices in the business.

Through the focus groups, they determined that there were several measures of quality that needed to be added to their current curriculum. They made changes to the curriculum based on this evidence. They started gathering additional evidence of student learning in the new curriculum. They found that by participating in an opera, or as part of the stage crew, students were able to apply the knowledge in their classes more effectively. The faculty decided on an action plan that included regular focus group sessions with follow-up opportunities for faculty reflection on the comments that the stakeholders provided. As a result of their efforts, the school returned to their national reputation for excellence in two years.

You should also keep in mind that these continuous process methods can be used to address areas in research, service, and business practices. The most important point is to determine the area(s) for improvement and then use the appropriate tools and strategies to raise them to the next level.

Conclusion

This chapter has focused on the need for assessment and continuous improvement as a means of confronting the difficult issues of access, affordability, accountability, and competitive advantage. The external forces of change surrounding a university have made their impact at the institutional and departmental levels. We have seen that for many schools assessment is already required by accrediting bodies and professional organizations. We have also seen that the economic realities of our time mandate that we leverage our resources in a manner that provides added value to students.

We have discussed methods for ascertaining the level of commitment to continuous improvement in your department by observing the levels of engagement of both faculty and students. The learning environment thrives where students own their acquisition of knowledge, are aware of the connectedness of learning and pursue it in active ways, and where faculty are energized by their work. We discussed the three levels of assessment in the department: student learning, faculty effectiveness, and program effectiveness. The reasons for faculty engagement in improvement processes are varied, but an understanding of basic human motivation will be an aid in determining the best motivators for your department. Wergin (2003) suggests that faculty are engaged when they perceive that they are doing "meaningful work." Key to seeing their work as meaningful is seeing evidence of contribution and improvement, which can be developed through assessment. Finally, we discussed key process indicators for a department and how those indicators are established.

Assessment, continuous improvement, and accountability have fundamentally altered the conditions under which contemporary colleges and universities operate. To some they might represent a form of bureaucratic interference in the autonomous operation of the academy. To many others, however, they represent important opportunities to innovate and improve.

As you consider ways that you can foster a culture of continuous improvement, you might wish to think about your responses to the following questions:

- How does your department define quality?
- How is it measured?

- What are the highest priority improvements that will position the department for the future?
- What methods will you use to accomplish your goals?

Suggested Resources

Bryan, C., & Clegg, K. (Eds.). (2006). *Innovative assessment in higher education*. New York, NY: Routledge.

Throughout higher education, assessment is changing, driven by increased class size, changing curricula, and the need to support students better. At the same time, assessment regulations and external quality assurance demands are constraining assessment options. This book is about the difficult process of changing assessment in sometimes unhelpful contexts.

Glickman, T. S., & White, S. C. (Eds.). (2007). *New directions for higher education: No. 137. Managing for innovation*. San Francisco, CA: Jossey-Bass.

This volume discusses innovations in higher education related to the application of the Baldrige Model, Universal Design across the Curriculum, the Challenge of Leadership Development, Linking Accreditation Standards and the Malcolm Baldrige Criteria, Information Technology, and Implementation for the Future.

Hernon, P., & Dugan, R. E. (Eds.). (2004). *Outcomes assessment in higher education: Views and perspectives*. Westport, CT: Libraries Unlimited.

This is a compendium of brief articles on various aspects of accreditation and assessment by well-recognized authors.

Massick, S. J. (Ed.). (1998). *Assessment in higher education: Issues of access, quality, student development and public policy*. Mahwah, NJ: Lawrence Erlbaum.

This volume discusses higher education problems and practices. It addresses such issues as equity of access and fairness in assessment and the politics of accountability, as well as concerns for student development and improved teaching.

Ramsden, P. (2003). *Learning to teach in higher education*. New York, NY: Routledge.

This book can help improve teaching with tools and resources to enhance teacher performance. The message of this classic text is simple: To become a good teacher, first you must understand your students' experiences of learning.

Sedlacek, W. E. (2004). *Beyond the big test: Noncognitive assessment in higher education*. San Francisco, CA: Jossey-Bass.

William E. Sedlacek, one of the nation's leading authorities on the topic of noncognitive assessment, challenges the use of the SAT and other standardized tests as the sole assessment tool for college and university admissions. In this book Sedlacek presents a noncognitive assessment method that can be used in concert with standardized tests. This assessment measures what students know by evaluating what they can do and how they deal with a wide range of problems in different contexts.

13

Build an Agenda

*I enjoy seeing the progress of faculty in their careers,
building up the department, and being told I'm
appreciated.*
              —A chair of agriculture at a research university

*It's important to recognize that chairs have power—
maybe more perceived than real. They can do almost
anything if they are supported by the faculty.*
    —A chair of communications at a comprehensive college

Our discussion has focused on building a positive work environment for faculty, and it began, in Part I, with your own self-development as a chair. It continued in a departmental context with your role as an academic leader. Finally, the building of a positive work environment for faculty was linked to your ability to establish sound rapport through good interpersonal relations. These strategies, as we call them, were applied in Part II to faculty undergoing predictable growth phases in their careers. These phases related to faculty needs: for orienting and adjusting to new departments; developing as effective teachers and scholars; refocusing of efforts at mid-career to better contribute to departments; solving personal issues that detract from overall individual and departmental performance; responding to technological developments; dealing with resource constraints; and maintaining quality. Phases such as these provide fertile opportunity for chairpersons to apply the strategies introduced in this book.

In this chapter, we synthesize the strategies into an overall framework for building a positive work environment for faculty. This framework has four key dimensions: develop *people*, consider the institutional *context*, acknowledge the *process*, and make a difference in *outcomes*.

Four Dimensions of the Building Process

1. Be Sensitive to the Developmental Growth of People and the Organization

A developmental perspective is based on the premise that individuals grow and develop professionally in response to changes in their personal lives and their work environments. We recommend that this perspective become an integral focus in your department. It could appear as an agenda item for your next departmental meeting. It might be discussed when faculty assignments are made. A growth perspective can pervade all aspects of departmental work.

Think in terms of the career phases of faculty. The needs of beginning staff differ from those of more senior, experienced staff. Faculty begin a career experiencing personal needs of adjusting, belonging, identifying, and learning about the new work environment. They might find success as teachers or scholars, or they might encounter setbacks. They struggle with student evaluations; they lecture over the heads of students; they become devastated by negative feedback about their teaching; they revel in the joys of teaching. In the research area, they might struggle with negative comments by reviewers; lack a focused line of research or continuity in their scholarship; misplace their priorities, thereby jeopardizing their chances for tenure or promotion; or publish a seminal work.

By mid- and late career, the survival question is no longer germane as they become promoted and tenured. But new difficulties and opportunities arise as their level of performance varies. New interests develop. Faculty surpass one benchmark and consider the next. They renegotiate the psychological contract with chairs. Classroom syllabi may no longer be relevant; few research studies might be undertaken because of increased interests in campus committee work or teaching. Personal issues related to health problems might interfere with their departmental performance.

To better understand faculty experiences at different stages of an academic career, a chair can turn to Baldwin and Blackburn's (1981) outline of the five stages of an academic career (i.e., assistant professors in the first three years of teaching, assistant professors with more than three years of teaching, associate professors, full professors with more than five years before retirement, and full professors within five years of retirement) in addition to considering faculty experiences such as career ambitions, enthusiasm, adjustments, disappointments, and familiarity with the organization.

Chairs experience professional change and growth, too. They go through phases in their careers, including entry-level socialization and learning about the position, establishing rapport with faculty and other unit administrators, attempting to reach long-range goals for the department and its people, and a phasing-out period that includes a resocialization to the faculty role or accepting more senior administrative posts. While not well detailed in the scholarly literature about chairing a department, these phases are predictable and represent times for chairs to reflect on their own progress and goals. Schein's (1978) stages in the career cycle offer insight into the general issues and specific tasks to be confronted. Schein's stages parallel the experiences of chairs, such as entry into the world of work, basic training, full membership in early- and mid-career, mid-career crisis, late-career nonleadership and leadership, and decline and disengagement leading to retirement.

The department, too, undergoes organizational growth. Organizational theorists talk about three stages in organizational development: creation and early development, transformations, and decline and termination (Kimberly & Miles, 1980). Undoubtedly, academic departments as formal organizations experience predictable growth phases. This suggests that individuals in departments acknowledge changes that are occurring, actively discuss them, and recognize that units do not remain static and unchanging. Chairpersons might ask themselves the following questions:

- Do I adjust my strategies to the needs of faculty at different stages of their careers?
- How am I growing and developing professionally?
- How is our department changing and developing?

2. Understand the Departmental, Institutional, and Disciplinary Context in Which Growth Occurs

Individual and departmental growth does not occur in a vacuum. Consider how the setting affects growth. Individuals respond to contexts differently, thus chairs need to continually assess the strengths, interests, and needs of faculty. But do not stop here: Match individual needs to departmental priorities, the institutional vision, and when important, to discipline needs.

As a case in point, this book describes several commonly occurring faculty situations with which chairpersons have to contend. Our choices are not meant to be exhaustive; faculty issues and situations are bounded by the context in which they arise. For example, in institutions with different missions and goals, faculty issues will vary. Bowen and Schuster (1986) discuss the different personal, educational, and world outlooks of individuals from different disciplines and differentiated institutional groups based on college values and goals. In our study, college teaching issues surfaced more in our analysis of community colleges, liberal arts schools, and comprehensive institutions. Not surprisingly, scholarly research questions arose far more often in our interviews with chairs at research universities. The strategies that chairs use might be discipline or field specific. Chairs in the hard or physical sciences are more concerned about funds for establishing laboratories and equipment purchases. Psychology chairs spoke more frequently than their peers about the interpersonal processes involved in helping faculty. In short, the context in which chairpersons assess and attempt to meet the needs of faculty is highly important to the strategies that are chosen and their likely success.

Strategies presented in this *Handbook* will certainly work well in one-on-one interactions with faculty, but they can also be used effectively in interactions with faculty in a group setting. Chairs discussed both approaches. Among the possibilities for one-one-one opportunities are:

- Informal day-to-day interactions
- Annual performance reviews at the end of the year
- Helping faculty establish goals for the year
- Social gatherings

In addition, chairs can have a positive affect on the entire department by:

- Sharing their vision at departmental meetings
- Creating an atmosphere where the vision is actively explored through consensus-building discussions and action planning
- Using an external facilitator to stimulate discussion or convening a departmental roundtable discussion
- Discussing what constitutes good teaching, research, or service in the department
- Identifying the best approaches to advocacy for the entire department, using realistic, specific language

Undoubtedly, the repertoire of involvement depends on time, individual style, and the willingness of faculty and the entire department to engage in open discussions of topics related to their performance and that of their departments. Chairs of departments that have a positive outlook seek approaches to broaden their involvement and recognize individual and departmental opportunities to make an impact. Chairs might ask themselves:

- In what ways do I assess the individual needs of my faculty?
- To which important departmental, institutional, or disciplinary priorities must I link these needs?
- When do I interact with faculty individually? How can these opportunities make a positive impact?
- When do I interact with the entire faculty? How can these opportunities make a positive impact?

3. Acknowledge that Building Is a Process

This orientation to leading as a process means that faculty change is a growth process that involves identifiable stages in which chairs can intervene and assist. Given the complexity of human nature, chairs need to assess carefully where each faculty member is in terms of career development and employ intervention strategies best suited to the individual and the context. When behaviors are more entrenched or chronic, chairs might need to adopt the long view. The keys to success in such cases are: take appropriate action, and be prepared to stay the course.

As we reviewed the process used by exemplary chairs, we advocated a four-step model that typified the approaches employed by experienced chairs in our study:

- Detect the signs of faculty needs
- Explore the options individually with the person
- Collaboratively develop a plan for action
- Enact the plan and monitor its results

This model reinforces a "systems" approach often found in the change literature. For example, Kirkpatrick (1985) advances a slightly more elaborate seven-step model that managers might use to bring about change in workers: determine the need or desire for a change, prepare a tentative plan, analyze probable reactions, make a final decision, establish a timetable, communicate the change, and implement the change.

Regardless of the model chosen, everyone acknowledges that changing someone else's behavior is difficult. You need to enter the process fully aware that individuals do not change until they are ready to do so. You cannot expect a 100% success rate. Chairs should look for small signs of success, incremental changes. As a chairperson, you should consider whether the individual whom you want to assist will accept your help. Maybe someone else is more appropriate (e.g., a fellow faculty member, a chaplain, an employee assistance counselor, a consultant from the faculty development center). Finally, recognize that the process of helping faculty will take your time, energy, and commitment. We can all identify with the chorus in Act II of Gilbert and Sullivan's *The Pirates of Penzance*, where they sing "a policeman's lot is not a happy one." When contemplating an intervention strategy with someone who is experiencing difficulty, you might ask yourself five important questions:

- What options are available to me in this situation?
- What are the potential outcomes of an intervention?
- What are the consequences of not proceeding?
- What steps should I follow?
- What assistance or support will I require?

4. Recognize that Chairs Can Make a Difference

Several positive outcomes should result from chairs adopting the strategies suggested by experienced chairs and developed in this *Handbook*. Chairs should acquire the self-confidence to initiate an agenda that is focused on continuous improvement and demonstrated results. In the process, individual faculty members should receive guidance as they progress through the stages of their careers. Finally, departments should become more cohesive and focused as they pursue their educational missions. As shown in Table 13.1, faculty might experience outcomes in relation to the chairperson's self-development, the chair acting as an academic leader, the interpersonal relations between chairs and faculty, and the processes used to bring about or address faculty issues. When thinking about the importance of maintaining a developmental focus, chairs might ask themselves:

- How does my own growth and development affect faculty?
- How am I serving as a leader in the department?
- How do I relate to faculty interpersonally?
- How do my growth, leadership, and interpersonal skills affect the process I am using to bring about change in individual faculty and in the department?

Table 13.1. Faculty outcomes.

Chairs . . .	Faculty Members . . .
Role model a balance between personal and professional life. Take time out for leisure activities. Realize that faculty will accept this time out as valid.	Learn how to create balance in their own lives. It is especially important for new faculty who are under pressure to perform.
Spend time learning about faculty interests, needs, and aspirations.	Feel they are valued, being heard, being helped.
Seek out other chairs and individuals on campus for insight into addressing faculty needs.	View assistance as positive. Create openness in the department where faculty can ask for assistance.
Learn the strengths and weaknesses of senior administrators.	Experience a chair who can be an effective advocate with administration for their needs.
Demonstrate academic vitality by remaining active in their fields.	See the chair as vital and interested in intellectual endeavors.

Chairs . . .	Faculty Members . . .
Help build a focus for the department and keep it before the faculty.	Feel that they can contribute to the focus. They recognize what will be rewarded, what the institution values, and acquire a sense of community.
Spend time carefully building faculty ownership of ideas.	Feel they are heard, listened to. They support departmental concepts or ideas.
Do not view change as immediate; instead, view change as evolutionary, incremental.	Are not suddenly jolted out of their usual patterns. They feel that change is of their own making.
Are aware of faculty needs for resources, information, and time off to pursue individual professional interests.	Feel supported. Welcome information and opportunities where they can regroup or pursue their favorite projects.
Consciously build a faculty data system to respond to requests in a timely fashion.	Might not acknowledge the need for this system but understand the importance of information about conveying their accomplishments to others.
Let faculty express their ideas freely, do not stifle ideas, and do not personalize criticism.	Are encouraged to trust and to be open with chairs and with other faculty in the department.
Spend time listening to faculty in one-on-one situations.	Feel important, feel that needs will be heard even if they are not addressed.

Chairs . . .	Faculty Members . . .
Help faculty set goals at the beginning of the year and review accomplishments of the goals with faculty at the end of the year.	Have an opportunity to talk about their professional careers with the chair and discuss personal and professional needs; have an opportunity at the end of the year to reflect on progress.
Are willing to provide both positive and negative feedback to faculty about performance.	Hear about both strengths and areas for improvement.
Actively advocate for faculty needs and interests with senior administrators on campus.	Feel that the chair is their advocate or protector.
Continually improve as scholars or teachers so they can be good role models and mentors for faculty.	Realize that the chair shares similar values; that the chair can provide assistance, even serve as a collaborator in teaching or research.
Take time from a busy schedule to appreciate faculty, praise their work, and acknowledge their areas of strength.	Feel good about their job and about themselves.
Adapt strategies to specific faculty needs.	Feel respected as individuals.
View faculty assistance as a process, a series of steps that unfold in a linear or nonlinear fashion.	Slowly work toward goals, begin making changes; hopefully do not regress.

Chairs . . .	Faculty Members . . .
Recognize that not all individuals are open to assistance; some people will not change.	Need to help themselves.
Keep abreast of technology developments that support faculty and student work.	Bring forward the most critical and cost-effective technology solutions.
Provide opportunities for faculty to acquire skills in using new technology applications.	Seek out and attend training sessions focused on the most productive technologies.
Consider ways to deploy technology to streamline administrative systems.	Consider ways to deploy technology to make teaching and research more efficient.
Develop a plan with faculty to allow for a transparent and systematic process for adoption of technology.	Participate in the creation of a technology plan that meets the highest needs of the department.
Clarify the extent of responsibility and accountability for budget development and management.	Be aware of the limits of fixed and discretionary spending in the department.
Anticipate consequences of budget reductions, personnel, and resource allocation.	Be aware of pressures caused by persistent budget constraints and engage the chair and colleagues in constructive discussions.
Engage faculty in discussions of the potential to increase external sources of funding.	Be willing to seek external funding through grants and donations, wherever appropriate.

Chairs . . .	Faculty Members . . .
Focus the department's efforts on quality, innovation, and results, and ensure that the proper metrics are in place to measure performance in these three critical areas.	Focus on quality, innovation, and results in individual professional endeavors, employ appropriate activity metrics, and contribute results to the department's overall accountability framework.
Read through these recommendations and actively work to incorporate them into their style.	Become more satisfied, productive, motivated, departmentally and institutionally oriented, and feel good about their work.

Implementing the Agenda

- *Consider starting an orientation program* for chairpersons on your campus if one does not already exist. Individuals typically learn the role from practical experience, and veteran chairs have much to offer in the way of practical tips. Ask these veterans about the strategies they use to address difficult faculty problems.
- *Read books about human developmental needs* so that you can recognize the needs of faculty in various stages of their careers. Granted, such reading might be outside your academic area, but the ideas might be useful as you work with faculty at different points in their academic lives.[1]
- *Read books on serving others and other-centered leadership.* These skills are useful when working with faculty, who are self-sufficient professionals in their own right.
- *Write into your job description the responsibility to assist faculty in their professional growth* so that you consciously allocate time for this activity. Chairs can be weighed

down by numerous responsibilities related to evaluating faculty, preparing reports, and putting out fires. Consider faculty growth as an equally important responsibility.

- *Develop your own set of faculty-oriented goals.* Identify the primary goals you have for helping faculty during the academic year. Share these goals with faculty during beginning-of-year or end-of-year reviews.
- *Attend workshops on interpersonal skills*, especially those that review good consultative skills such as active listening, feedback, coping, and confrontation. Participate in activities where you can observe or listen to your approach through role-playing, videotaping, or audio recording.
- *Create a career plan for your own professional future.* Identify 5- and 10-year objectives. Share this plan with others whom you respect and ask for their feedback.
- *Renegotiate your own contract for effort and rewards* with faculty so that they see you not only as a faculty "evaluator" but also as an individual who facilitates the careers of your faculty.
- *Recognize that some strategies take less time to carry out than others.* Look at the "Topical Index to Strategies" in Appendix B at the end of this book.
- *Celebrate the job of establishing a positive department for faculty.* Recognize that the exemplary chairs in our project often considered the growth and development of their faculty as a major satisfaction in their job.

Conclusion

The literature on academic leadership, our personal experiences as academic administrators, our interviews with seasoned department chairs, and our interactions with chairs in numerous workshop settings have combined to reinforce for us that chairs occupy exceedingly busy and demanding positions in their varied institutions. These positions are located at the nexus of important change in our institutions, and, hence, the role of the chair has become far more critical as the forces of change in higher education have accelerated in recent years. Against this fast-paced and dynamic backdrop, most chairs enter their positions with little awareness of what the job really entails and even less preparation for what awaits them in the position.

The plan of this *Handbook* was deliberately simple. Provide chairs, in the first part, with a realistic view of the challenges they will typically confront, and offer 15 practical strategies they can employ in the process of supporting both their own and their departments' development. Provide them, in the second part, with specific techniques for dealing with myriad issues related to faculty performance in several areas, including orientation, teaching, scholarship, professional growth and career development, and personal issues of faculty. In addition, the second part also provided chairs with ways to deal with the pressures created by accelerating developments in technology, changing funding arrangements, and increasing requirements for assessment and accountability.

While each of these strategies and their related tactics are vitally important to the success of chairs and their departments, their effectiveness relies, in a very real sense, on the fundamental values and beliefs that guide the actions of chairs. As you embark, therefore, on the task of implementing the strategies outlined in this *Handbook*, you might wish to consider the following axioms drawn from our own experience and from advice shared with us by academic leaders over the years.[2]

- *Always act with integrity.* You will be forgiven a lack of administrative knowledge or skills but seldom a lack of character.
- *Build trust.* Almost anything will work when enough trust is present, but without it almost nothing will work.

- *Avoid acting impulsively.* Listen carefully to all viewpoints and reflect on what you hear before making important decisions.
- *Act in a consistent manner.* Make your word your bond; if you say you are going to do something, then do it.
- *Avoid bias in dealing with people.* As difficult as it might be at times, everyone deserves equitable treatment.
- *Maintain confidences.* Remember the old saying that confidentiality in an academic institution often simply means telling one person at a time.
- *Accept criticism and admit mistakes.* As Mark Twain once remarked in another context, "It will gratify some people and astonish the rest."
- *Adopt a positive, purposeful outlook.* Without a sense of purpose, it is difficult to motivate yourself, let alone those you lead.
- *Communicate, communicate, communicate.* It is not what people know but what they do not know that causes problems.
- *Know when it is time to leave.* Set goals, measure progress, seek feedback, and decide when it is time to look for new challenges and opportunities.

The success of our graduates, the reputation of our institutions, and the prosperity of our nation rely on the excellence of the teaching, scholarship, and service of our faculty. No one plays a more important role than department chairs in attracting, socializing, and supporting faculty as they progress through their careers and make essential contributions to their students, their professions, and their departments.

To those chairs who have already performed so capably in their challenging roles, we offer our sincere appreciation; to those about to make their contributions, we offer our best wishes for success.

Endnotes

1. You might wish to consult the Suggested Resources sections, particularly in Part I of the *Handbook*, where you will find both classic and contemporary references to the human development literature.

2. The inspiration for creating this set of axioms derives from a list created by Walker in *The Effective Administrator* (1986). The authors also wish to acknowledge the influence of Gardner's *On Leadership* (1990), especially with respect to his advice on the importance of trust.

References

Andersen, K. J. (1977). In defense of departments. In D. E. McHenry & Associates, *Academic departments: Problems, variations, and alternatives* (pp. 1–12). San Francisco, CA: Jossey-Bass.

Bain, K. (2004). *What the best college teachers do*. Cambridge, MA: Harvard University Press.

Baldwin, R. T., & Blackburn, R. G. (1981, November/December). The academic career as a developmental process: Implications for higher education. *Journal of Higher Education, 52*(6), 598–614.

Barr, M. J. (2002). *Jossey-Bass academic administrator's guide to budgets and financial management*. San Francisco, CA: Jossey-Bass.

Barrow, S., & Davenport, J. (2002). *"The employer brand," People in business*. Unpublished manuscript.

Bennis, W. (1973, May). An O.D. expert in the cat bird's seat. *Journal of Higher Education, 44*(5), 389–398.

Bennis, W., & Nanus, B. (1985). *Leaders: Strategies for taking charge*. New York, NY: HarperCollins.

Bess, J. L. (1982). The motivation to teach: Meanings, messages, and morals. In J. T. Bess (Ed.), *New directions for teaching and learning: No. 10. Motivating professors to teach effectively* (pp. 99–107). San Francisco, CA: Jossey-Bass.

Blackburn, R. T., Bober, A., O'Donnel, C., & Pellino, G. (1980). *Project for faculty development program evaluation: Final report*. Ann Arbor, MI: University of Michigan, Center for the Study of Higher Education.

Bland, C. J., & Bergquist, W. H. (1997). *The vitality of senior faculty members: Snow on the roof—fire in the furnace* (ASHE-ERIC Higher Education Report, Vol. 25, No. 7). Washington, DC: The George Washington University, Graduate School of Education and Human Development.

Bland, C. J., & Risbey, K. R. (2006, July). Faculty development programs. *Effective Practices for Academic Leaders, 1*(7), 1–16.

Bland, C. J., Weber-Main, A. M., Lund, S. M., & Finstad, D. A. (2005). *The research-productive department: Strategies from departments that excel*. Bolton, MA: Anker.

Boice, R. (1982). Counseling colleagues. *Personnel and Guidance Journal, 61*(4), 239–241.

Bowen, H. R., & Schuster, J. H. (1986). *American professors: A national resource imperiled*. New York, NY: Oxford University Press.

Boyer, E. L. (1990). *Scholarship reconsidered: Priorities of the professoriate*. Princeton, NJ: The Carnegie Foundation for the Advancement of Teaching.

Brammer, L. M. (1979). *The helping relationship: Process and skills* (2nd ed.). Englewood Cliffs, NJ: Prentice-Hall.

Bridges, W. (1980). *Transitions: Making sense of life's changes*. Reading, MA: Addison-Wesley.

Brown, B. E. (2006, September). Supporting and retaining early-career faculty. *Effective Practices for Academic Leaders, 1*(9), 1–16.

Brown, D. G. (Ed.). (2003). *Ubiquitous computing: The universal use of computers on college campuses*. Bolton, MA: Anker.

Brown, J. D. (1977). Departmental and university leadership. In D. E. McHenry & Associates, *Academic departments: Problems, variations, and alternatives* (pp. 189–205). San Francisco, CA: Jossey-Bass.

Bryan, C., & Clegg, K. (Eds.). (2006). *Innovative assessment in higher education*. New York, NY: Routledge.

Buckingham, M., & Coffman, C. (1999). *First, break all the rules: What the world's greatest managers do differently*. New York, NY: Simon & Schuster.

Carroll, J. B., & Gmelch, W. H. (1994, Summer/Fall). Department chairs' perceptions of the relative importance of their duties. *Journal for Higher Education Management, 10*(1), 49–63.

Chait, R. (2002). The "academic revolution" revisited. In S. J. Brint (Ed.), *The future of the city of intellect: The changing American university* (pp. 294–391). Stanford, CA: Stanford University Press.

Cheldelin, S. I., & Lucas, A. F. (2004). *Jossey-Bass academic administrator's guide to conflict resolution*. San Francisco, CA: Jossey-Bass.

Chu, D. (2006). *The department chair primer: Leading and managing academic departments*. Bolton, MA: Anker.

Conklin, K., & Reindl, T. (2004, February 13). To keep America competitive, states and colleges must work together. *The Chronicle of Higher Education*, p. B20.

Creswell, J. W. (1985). *Faculty research performance: Lessons from the sciences and the social sciences* (ASHE/ERIC Higher Education Report No. 4). Washington, DC: Association for the Study of Higher Education.

Creswell, J. W., & Brown, M. L. (1992, Fall). How chairpersons enhance faculty research: A grounded theory study. *Review of Higher Education, 16*(1), 41–62.

Creswell, J. W., Wheeler, D. W., Seagren, A. T., Egly, N. J., & Beyer, K. D. (1990). *The academic chairperson's handbook*. Lincoln, NE: University of Nebraska Press.

Csikszentmihalyi, M. (1982). Intrinsic motivation and effective teaching: A flow analysis. In J. T. Bess (Ed.), *New directions for teaching and learning: No. 10. Motivating professors to teach effectively* (pp. 15–26). San Francisco, CA: Jossey-Bass.

Csikszentmihalyi, M. (1990). *Flow: The psychology of optimal experience*. New York, NY: Harper & Row.

Curry, T. H. (2006). Faculty performance reviews. *Effective Practices for Academic Leaders, 1*(2), 1–16.

Curtis, J. W. (Ed.). (2005). *New directions for higher education: No. 130. The challenge of balancing faculty careers and family work.* San Francisco, CA: Jossey-Bass.

Davis, B. G. (1993). *Tools for teaching.* San Francisco, CA: Jossey-Bass.

Derr, W. D. (2005, March/April). Envisioning EAP's future by reflecting on its past. *Behavioral Health Management, 25*(2), 13–18.

Diamond, R. M. (Ed.). (2002). *Field guide to academic leadership.* San Francisco, CA: Jossey-Bass.

Duderstadt, J. J., Atkins, D. E., & Van Houweling, D. (2002). *Higher education in the digital age: Technology issues and strategies for American colleges and universities.* Westport, CT: Praeger.

Eble, K. (1986). Chairpersons and faculty development. *The Department Advisor, 1*(4), 1–5.

Eble, K. E. (1998). *The craft of teaching* (2nd ed.). San Francisco, CA: Jossey-Bass.

Eble, K. E., & McKeachie, W. J. (1985). *Improving undergraduate education through faculty development.* San Francisco, CA: Jossey-Bass.

Feldman, K. A. (1988, December). Effective college teaching from the students' and faculty's view: Matched or mismatched priorities? *Research in Higher Education, 28*(4), 291–329.

Fischer, K. (2005, December 2). Louisiana lawmakers slash college spending. *The Chronicle of Higher Education,* p. A21.

Fischer, K. (2006, January 13). State spending on colleges bounces back. *The Chronicle of Higher Education,* p. A1.

Fisher, R., & Ury, W. (1981). *Getting to yes: Negotiating agreement without giving in.* Boston, MA: Houghton Mifflin.

Friedman, D. E., Rimsky, C., & Johnson, A. A. (1996). *College and university reference guide to work-family programs: Report on a collaborative study*. New York, NY: Families and Work Institute.

Furniss, W. T. (1981). *Reshaping faculty careers*. Washington, DC: American Council on Education.

Gaff, J. G., Pruitt-Logan, A. S., & Weibl, R. A. (2000). *Building the faculty we need: Colleges and universities working together*. Washington, DC: Association of American Colleges and Universities.

Gappa, J. M., Austin, A. E., & Trice, A. G. (2007). *Rethinking faculty work: Higher education's strategic imperative*. San Francisco, CA: Jossey-Bass.

Gappa, J. M., & MacDermid, S. M. (1997). *Work, family, and the faculty career* (New Pathways Working Paper Series, Inquiry #8). Washington, DC: American Association for Higher Education.

Gardner, J. W. (1990). *On leadership*. New York, NY: The Free Press.

Glickman, T. S., & White, S. C. (Eds.). (2007). *New directions for higher education: No. 137. Managing for innovation*. San Francisco, CA: Jossey-Bass.

Gmelch, W. H. (2006, January). Stress management strategies for academic leaders. *Effective Practices for Academic Leaders, 1*(1), 2.

Gmelch, W. H., & Burns, J. S. (1993, June). The cost of academic leadership: Department chair stress. *Innovative Higher Education, 17*(4), 259–270.

Gmelch, W. H., & Miskin, V. D. (2004). *Chairing an academic department* (2nd ed.). Madison, WI: Atwood.

Gmelch, W. H., & Schuh, J. H. (Eds.). (2004). *New directions for higher education: No. 126. The life cycle of a department chair*. San Francisco, CA: Jossey-Bass.

Halford, A. (1994, February). *Faculty morale: Enhancing it in spite of diminishing resources and challenges*. Paper presented at the 3rd annual International Conference for Community College Chairs, Deans, and Other Instructional Leaders, Phoenix, AZ.

Hecht, I. W. D. (2006, March). Becoming a department chair. *Effective Practices for Academic Leaders, 1*(3), 1–16.

Hecht, I. W. D., Higgerson, M. L., Gmelch, W. H., & Tucker, A. (1999). *The department chair as academic leader*. Phoenix, AZ: American Council on Education/Oryx Press.

Heider, J. (1985). *The Tao of leadership: Leadership strategies for a new age*. New York, NY: Bantam.

Henry, R. J. (Ed.). (2006). *New directions for higher education: No. 134. Transitions between faculty and administrative careers*. San Francisco, CA: Jossey-Bass.

Hernon, P., & Dugan, R. E. (Eds.). (2004). *Outcomes assessment in higher education: Views and perspectives*. Westport, CT: Libraries Unlimited.

Howe, N., & Strauss, W. (2000). *Millennials rising: The next great generation*. New York, NY: Vintage.

Jones, D. (2006). *State shortfalls projected to continue despite economic gains: Long-term prospects for higher education no brighter*. San Jose, CA: National Center for Public Policy and Higher Education.

Kanter, R. M. (1981). Quality of work life and work behavior in academia. *National Forum, 60*(4), 35–39.

Keeling, R. P. (Ed.). (2004). *Learning reconsidered 1: A campus-wide focus on the student experience*. Washington, DC: American College Personnel Association & National Association of Student Personnel Administrators.

Kerr, C. (2002). Shock wave II: An introduction to the twenty-first century. In S. J. Brint (Ed.), *The future of the city of intellect: The changing American university* (pp. 1–19). Stanford, CA: Stanford University Press.

Kimberly, J. R. & Miles, R. H. (1980). *The organizational life cycle: Issues in the creation, transformation, and decline of organizations*. San Francisco, CA: Jossey-Bass.

Kimble, G. A. (1979). *A departmental chair's survival manual.* New York, NY: Wiley.

Kirkpatrick, D. L. (1985). *How to manage change effectively: Approaches, methods, and case examples.* San Francisco, CA: Jossey-Bass.

Kouzes, J. M., & Posner, B. Z. (2003). *Jossey-Bass academic administrator's guide to exemplary leadership.* San Francisco, CA: Jossey-Bass.

Kouzes, J. M., & Posner, B. Z. (2007). *The leadership challenge* (4th ed.). San Francisco, CA: Jossey-Bass.

Kübler-Ross, E. (1975). *Death: The final stage of growth.* New York, NY: Simon & Schuster.

Leaming, D. R. (2007). *Academic leadership: A practical guide to chairing the department* (2nd ed.). Bolton, MA: Anker.

Lees, N. D. (2006). *Chairing academic departments: Traditional and emerging expectations.* Bolton, MA: Anker.

Leslie, D. W. (2006). *Faculty careers and flexible employment.* Retrieved November 1, 2007, from www.tiaa-crefinstitute.org/research/policy/pol010106.html

Leslie, D. W., & Fretwell, E. K., Jr. (1996). *Wise moves in hard times: Creating and managing resilient colleges and universities.* San Francisco, CA: Jossey-Bass.

Lewis, K. G. (1988). Individual consultation: Its importance to faculty development programs. In K. G. Lewis & J. T. P. Lunde (Eds.), *Face to face: A sourcebook of individual consultation techniques for faculty/instructional developers* (pp. 1–5). Stillwater, OK: New Forums Press.

Licata, C. M., & Morreale, J. C. (2006). *Post-tenure faculty review and renewal III: Outcomes and impacts.* Bolton, MA: Anker.

Lick, D. W. (2002). Leadership and change. In R. M. Diamond (Ed.), *Field guide to academic leadership* (pp. 27–48). San Francisco, CA: Jossey-Bass.

Lucas, A. F. (1994). *Strengthening departmental leadership: A team-building guide for chairs in colleges and universities.* San Francisco, CA: Jossey-Bass.

Lucas, A. F. (2000). *Leading academic change: Essential roles for department chairs.* San Francisco, CA: Jossey-Bass.

Mager, R. F., & Pipe, P. (1970). *Analyzing performance problems.* Belmont, CA: Fearon Pitman.

March, J. G. (1980, September). *How we talk and how we act: Administrative theory and administrative life.* Paper presented at the 7th David D. Henry Lecture on Administration, University of Illinois at Urbana–Champaign, Urbana, IL.

Massick, S. J. (Ed.). (1998). *Assessment in higher education: Issues of access, quality, student development and public policy.* Mahwah, NJ: Lawrence Erlbaum.

Massy, W. F. (1996, Winter). New thinking on academic restructuring. *Priorities, 6,* 1–16.

McCaffery, P. (2004). *The higher education manager's handbook: Effective leadership and management in colleges and universities.* New York, NY: Routledge.

McKeachie, W. J. (1999). *Teaching tips.* Boston, MA: Houghton Mifflin.

McKeachie, W. J., & Svinicki, M. (2006). *McKeachie's teaching tips: Strategies, research, and theory for college and university teachers* (12th ed.). Boston, MA: Houghton Mifflin.

McLaughlin, G. W., Montgomery, J. R., & Malpass, L. F. (1975). Selected characteristics, roles, goals, and satisfactions of department chairmen in state and land-grant institutions. *Research in Higher Education, 3*(3), 243–259.

Menges, R. J. (1991). The real world of teaching improvement: A faculty perspective. In M. Theall & J. Franklin (Eds.), *New directions for teaching and learning: No. 48. Effective practices for improving teaching* (pp. 21–37). San Francisco, CA: Jossey-Bass.

Miller, M. T., Benton, C. J., & Vacik, S. M. (1998, April–May). Managing scarce resources in the community college: Strategies for the department chair. *Community College Journal of Research and Practice, 22*(3), 203–211.

Morris, J. (2007). The current leadership crisis and thoughts on solutions. In T. C. Mack (Ed.), *Hopes and visions for the 21st century* (pp. 250–263). Bethesda, MD: World Future Society.

Mott, M. (1994, February). *The hunt for hidden resources: A chair's guide to finding campus support for faculty and staff development*. Paper presented at the 3rd International Conference for Community College Chairs, Deans, and Other Instructional Leaders, Phoenix, AZ.

Nanus, B. (1992). *Visionary leadership: Creating a compelling sense of direction for your organization*. San Francisco, CA: Jossey-Bass.

Nanus, B. (1995). *The vision retreat: A participant's workbook*. San Francisco, CA: Jossey-Bass.

Newman, F., Couturier, L., & Scurry, J. (2004). *The future of higher education: Rhetoric, reality, and the risks of the market*. San Francisco, CA: Jossey-Bass.

Oblinger, D. G., & Oblinger, J. L. (Eds.). (2005). *Educating the net generation*. Boulder, CO: EDUCAUSE.

O'Meara, K., & Rice, R. E. (2005). *Faculty priorities reconsidered: Rewarding multiple forms of scholarship*. San Francisco, CA: Jossey-Bass.

Pew Higher Education Roundtable. (1994). To dance with change. *Policy Perspectives, 5*(3), 1–12.

Ramsden, P. (2003). *Learning to teach in higher education*. New York, NY: Routledge.

Rice, R. E., Sorcinelli, M. D., & Austin, A. E. (2000). *Heeding new voices: Academic careers for a new generation* (New Pathways Working Paper Series, Inquiry #7). Washington, DC: American Association for Higher Education.

Rousseau, D. M. (1995). *Psychological contracts in organizations: Understanding written and unwritten agreements*. Thousand Oaks, CA: Sage.

Scanlon, W. F. (1986). *Alcoholism and drug abuse in the workplace: Employee assistance programs*. New York, NY: Praeger.

Schein, E. (1978). *Career dynamics: Matching individual and organizational needs.* Reading, MA: Addison-Wesley.

Seagren, A. T., Creswell, J. W., & Wheeler, D. W. (1993). *The department chair: New roles, responsibilities, and challenges.* Washington, DC: The George Washington University, Graduate School of Education and Human Development.

Sedlacek, W. E. (2004). *Beyond the big test: Noncognitive assessment in higher education.* San Francisco, CA: Jossey-Bass.

Seldin, P. (1980). *Successful faculty evaluation programs.* New York, NY: Coventry Press.

Seldin, P. (1993). *Improving and evaluating teaching.* Paper presented at the American Council on Education Department Chairs Seminar, Washington, DC.

Seldin, P. (1994). *Improving college teaching.* Paper presented at Hong Kong University, Hong Kong.

Shaw, R. (1995). Fund raising—An essential activity for all undergraduate department chairs. *Journal of College Science Teaching, 24*(5), 308.

Stein, S. A. (2002, September/October). Why work/life and EAP should be integrated. *Behavioral Health Management, 22*(5), 33–41.

Taylor-Way, D. (1988). Consultation with video: Memory management through stimulated recall. In K. G. Lewis & J. T. P. Lunde (Eds.), *Face to face: A sourcebook of individual consultation techniques for faculty/instructional developers* (pp. 159–191). Stillwater, OK: New Forums Press.

Thomas, J. R. (2006, May). Fostering scholarly research in departments and colleges. *Effective Practices for Academic Leaders, 1*(5), 1–16.

Thoreson, R. W., & Hosokawa, E. P. (1984). *Employee assistance programs in higher education: Alcohol, mental health and professional development programming for faculty and staff.* Springfield, IL: Charles C. Thomas.

TIAA-CREF Research Dialogue. (1988). *Employee assistance programs in educational institutions* (No. 16). New York, NY: TIAA-CREF Institute.

Tierney, W. G. (1998). On the road to recovery and renewal: Reinventing academe. In W. G. Tierney (Ed.), *The responsive university: Restructuring for high performance* (pp. 1–12). Baltimore, MD: The Johns Hopkins University Press.

Tierney, W. G. (2002). Mission and vision statements: An essential first step. In R. M. Diamond (Ed.), *Field guide to academic leadership* (pp. 49–58). San Francisco, CA: Jossey-Bass.

Tucker, A. (1984). *Chairing the academic department: Leadership among peers* (2nd ed.). New York, NY: American Council on Education/Macmillan.

Tucker, A. (1992). *Chairing the academic department: Leadership among peers* (3rd ed.). New York. NY: American Council on Education/Macmillan.

University of California–Los Angeles, Higher Education Research Institute. (1999). *The American college teacher: National norms 1998–1999 HERI faculty survey report.* Los Angeles, CA: Author.

U.S. Department of Education, Office of Educational Technology. (2004). *Toward a new golden age in American education: How the internet, the law and today's students are revolutionizing expectations.* Washington, DC: Author.

Walker, D. E. (1986). *The effective administrator: A practical approach to problem solving, decision making, and campus leadership.* San Francisco, CA: Jossey-Bass.

Weigel, V. B. (2001). *Deep learning for a digital age: Technology's untapped potential to enrich higher education.* San Francisco, CA: Jossey-Bass.

Wergin, J. F. (2003). *Departments that work: Building and sustaining cultures of excellence in academic programs.* Bolton, MA: Anker.

Wiggins, G., & McTighe, J. (2006). An introduction to understanding by design. In R. P. Keeling (Ed.), *Learning reconsidered 2: A practical guide to implementing a campus-wide focus on the student experience.* Washington, DC: American College Personnel Association, Association of College and University Housing Officers–International, Association of College Unions–International, National Academic Advising Association, National Association for Campus Activities, National Association of Student Personnel Administrators, and National Intramural–Recreational Sports Association.

Wolverton, M., Ackerman, R., & Holt, S. (2005, July). Preparing for leadership: What academic department chairs need to know. *Journal of Higher Education Policy and Management, 27*(2), 227–238.

Wolvoord, B. E., Carey, A. K., Smith, H. L., Soled, S. W., Way, P. K., & Zorn, D. (2000). *Academic departments: How they work, how they change* (ASHE-ERIC Higher Education Report, Vol. 27, No. 8). Washington, DC: The George Washington University, Graduate School of Education and Human Development.

Appendix A

The National Study and the Follow-Up Study

Strategies used by academic chairs in assisting faculty members to grow and develop professionally were examined in a three-year study begun in 1985. The research methodology was qualitative, with a semi-structured interview protocol and follow-up campus visits serving as the method for data collection. Sponsored by TIAA-CREF and supported financially by the Lilly Endowment, Inc., this national project involved 200 department chairs on 70 college and university campuses.

Chairpersons who served as subjects for our project represented a special sample. The individuals were nominated on their campuses by senior academic administrators and faculty development specialists (where the positions existed) for excelling in the professional growth assistance they provided to faculty.[1] These "excellent" chairs demonstrated distinguished records for supporting faculty members. They possessed strong interpersonal skills, encouraged faculty to participate in developmental activities, held the respect of colleagues as academic leaders and scholars, and understood the mission, direction, priorities, and orientation of the institutions they served. Fourteen percent of the chairs participating in the project were female and 86% were male. Participating chairpersons represented diverse disciplines. They were social scientists (e.g., economists, sociologists, psychologists, and anthropologists), natural scientists (e.g., physicists, chemists, medical scientists, and geologists), humanists and artists (e.g., theater directors, English and foreign language specialists, historians, and visual artists), and professionals (e.g., engineers, architects, and journalists).

The 70 campuses on which the 200 chairpersons were employed represented four of the major types of higher education institutions as classified by the Carnegie Foundation for the Advancement of Teaching: research universities, doctoral-granting institutions, comprehensive colleges, and liberal arts schools. Two-year campuses and specialized institutions were excluded.[2] Institutions were located in 33 states and included campuses along the Atlantic and Pacific coasts and in the South and Midwest.

The schools represented public and private campuses and included institutions with substantial enrollments of Native American, black, Hispanic, and female students. Some schools had negotiated collective bargaining agreements with their faculty members. Numbers of students enrolled ranged from approximately 600 to more than 40,000 students.

We conducted 45-minute telephone interviews with the 200 nominees and made eight campus visits to interview the chairs, their faculty members, faculty development specialists, and academic deans and other administrators to follow up on the telephone interviews.

Seven interviewers were trained in data gathering techniques. The interviewers maintained an ongoing dialogue concerning the inter-rater consistency of data recording and coding procedures. The analysis of interview data proceeded inductively, with applicable coding schemes unfolding as we listened to and read interview records and entered data on the computer. Analyses were assisted by use of the dBASE III-database and SPSS-X computer programs. The interviews, site visits, and consultation of related literature provided triangulation for the database. In the analysis used in this book, special emphasis has been placed on data derived from interview protocol questions concerning specific incidents of chairs helping a single faculty member in the department and the strategies that chairs would recommend to a new chairperson.

In 2004 the authors began to consider an update to the *Handbook* because there was mounting evidence that the challenges faced by department chairs were increasing and their responsibilities were expanding. The research team began by developing a semi-structured interview protocol that focused on eight themes: quality, culture, leadership, accountability, standards, advice, performance, and change. The group chose to expand the book's original scope by applying the Carnegie Classification and conducting interviews at both two- and four-year public and private institutions across all geographic regions of the United States as well as in representative regions of Canada.

In total, 47 institutions were identified as meeting the criteria related to four key areas of focus: quality, culture, leadership, and change. These institutions were selected from among those who participate in the Academic Quality Improvement Program (AQIP); those identified by Presidents of the National Association of State Universities and Land-Grant Colleges (NASULGC); and others who are generally recognized for their focus on quality of teaching. Eventually, interviews were conducted with 38 department chairs at 24 institutions. The interviews were tape recorded and transcribed. The data were analyzed using QSR N6 (V6.0) software. The results generated 76 nodes, which were coded and used to develop the four major thematic patterns: quality, culture, leadership, and change.

Of the chairpersons interviewed, 28 were employed in four-year public institutions, 6 worked in private institutions, and 4 worked in Canadian public institutions. Twenty-six chairpersons worked in four-year institutions, while 12 worked in two-year institutions. Twenty-three chairpersons were appointed, while 15 were elected. Their terms ranged from annual (six) to continuous (eight). They tended to be experienced faculty and chairs: Their average tenure in higher education was 23 years, and their average tenure as chairpersons was 8.6 years. They represented a broad spectrum of disciplines in physical and life sciences, mathematics, social sciences, and arts and humanities. They also represented a range of professional fields, including business, social work, education, and communications.

Endnotes

1. In conducting the research for the first edition we used the following question: "Please nominate three to five chairpersons (or their equivalents) on your campus who excel in assisting faculty grow and develop professionally."

2. We used the classification system advanced by the Carnegie Foundation for the Advancement of Teaching in the July 8, 1987, *Chronicle of Higher Education*.

Appendix B

Topical Index to Strategies

General Strategies

Everyday Strategies

Strategies for Refocusing Faculty Effort

Strategies for Addressing Personal Issues

Strategies for Building an Agenda

Index